Northeast Asia in 2030

Forging Ahead or Drifting Away?

ARI Monograph Series_ 31

NORTHEAST ASIA IN 2030

Forging Ahead or Drifting Away?

by Choi Byung-il

Asiatic Research Institute

| Contents |

Figures and Tables

List of Figures

List of Tables

Abbreviation and Acronym

AI	Artificial intelligence
AIIB	Asian Infrastructure Investment Bank
AMF	Asian Monetary Fund
APEC	Asia-Pacific Economic Cooperation
ASEAN	Association of Southeast Asian Nations
BIT	Bilateral Investment Treaty
CJK	China-Japan-Korea
CPTPP	Comprehensive and Progressive Agreement for TPP (Trans Pacific Partnership)
DDA	Doha Development Agenda
DPJ	Democratic Party of Japan
EAEP	East Asian Economic Partnership
ECCC	European Chamber of Commerce in China
EPA	Economic Partnership Agreement
EU	European Union
FDI	Foreign Direct Investment
FTA	Free Trade Agreement
G20	Group 20
G7	Group 7
GATS	General Agreement on Trade in Services
GATT	General Agreement on Tariffs and Trade
GDP	Gross Domestic Product
GVC	Global Value Chain
ICSID	International Centre for Settlement of Investment Disputes
ICT	Information and Communication Technology
IMF	International Monetary Fund
IPR	Intellectual property rights

ISDS	Investor-State Dispute Settlement
KORUS FTA	Korea-US Free Trade Agreement
LDP	Liberal Democratic Party
MAFF	Ministry of Agriculture, Forestry, and Fisheries
METI	Ministry of Economy, Trade, and Industry
MFN	Most Favored Nation
MOFAT	Ministry of Foreign Affairs and Trade
NAFTA	North American Free Trade Area
NT	National treatment
NTM	Non-Tariff Measure
NTR	Normal trading relations
OECD	Organization for Economic Cooperation and Development
OMT	Office of the Minister for Trade
PNTR	Permanent Normal Trade Relations
PPP	Purchasing Power Parity
RCEP	Regional Comprehensive Economic Partnership
SDF	Self-Defense Forces
SME	Small and Medium-sized Enterprise
SOEs	State-owned enterprises
SPS	Sanitary and phytosanitary measures and agreement
TBT	Technical Barriers to Trade
TCS	Trilateral Cooperation Secretariat
THAAD	Terminal High Altitude Area Defense
TPA	Trade Promotion Authority
TPP	Trans-Pacific Partnership
UNCITRAL	United Nations Commission on International Trade Law
USTR	United States Trade Representative
WTO	World Trade Organization

Foreword

East Asia's dynamic development after the Cold War has been influencing new changes in many areas, ranging from politics, diplomacy, economic order to culture, thoughts and religion. Such change is giving rise to transnational phenomena, highly complex and sensitive, which defies an easy account from study of individual sovereign states.

Especially in the case of Northeast Asia, on the rise are active transnational ideas and movements, which derive from geological proximity, common historical-cultural experience, and the need for cooperation and coexistence. In order to deepen the understanding of Northeast Asia and to offer new explanations and prospects, interdisciplinary research analyzing Northeast Asia as a whole is imperative.

The practical implications of Northeast Asian study are significant. Although Northeast Asia has underwent rapid change and growth, more so than any other part of the world, the region is still tied up in problems of modernity and legacies of the Cold War. The experience of imperialism and colonization in the early 20th century is still instilled in the memories of today's nations and public. The divide of North and South Korea, the lasting legacy of the Cold War, and the threat of North Korean nuclear weapons are the grave sources of insecurity in Northeast Asia. History disputes and territorial disputes remain as major obstacles in the way of Northeast Asia's peaceful development.

However, the uncomfortable historical experiences and current instability can, on the other hand, closely connect Northeast Asia's various components and establish a common base for problem solving. Northeast Asia has been a stage for confrontation and conflict, but it can be also a ground for peace and coexistence. Northeast Asian study should break away with subjective and emotional diagnosis and move towards more objective and rational analysis of Northeast Asia's realities, if it aims to rise up to the call of establishing a peaceful future.

As a representative Northeast Asia research center, Asiatic Research Institute (ARI) has played a leading role in Northeast Asian studies by producing a number of research achievements through interdisciplinary approach. Since its establishment in 1957, ARI has compiled a series of research, in fields of diplomatic documents from the Korean Empire, the Communist bloc, Northeast Asia, China, Korea and Japan, and Democracy. Through such efforts, ARI has dutifully acted its role as a university research center for the rigorous research of reality and forecast of desirable future directions. In 2008, ARI was selected as one of the recipient research institutes of the state-sponsored Humanities Korea (HK) Project for regional studies, obtaining a 10-year financial support from the government. Ever since, the Institute has been running a 10 year-long project under the research agenda of "Northeast Asia's transnational space: thought-society-culture-institution's interaction and reorganization." As an integral part of this project, ARI is now proud to publish the ARI Monograph Series on Northeast Asia.

It is my pleasure to present Northeast Asia in 2030: Forging Ahead and Drifting Away? by Choi Byung-il. In this book, Choi gives his analysis of the current status of Northeast Asia trade arrangements and offers policy suggestions for more stable, prosperous and inclusive future for Northeast Asia. The book is rather unique and differentiated from existing studies in the sense that the author has tried to integrate politics and economics with linking country-to-country aspect of the issue and within-the-country aspect of the same issue. The book is in the very spirit of interdisciplinary approach. Wish is that this book serves a fertile basis for serious debate and soul search for desirable yet realistic future course of Northeast Asia trade relations.

Lee Jong-Wha
Director
Asiatic Research Institute

Preface

"Do you think whether Korea will join the TPP?" In February 2013, I had a visitor from Canada, a high-ranking government official, who was coming to Korea to attend the inauguration ceremony of President Park Geun-hye. In my office, overlooking the National Assembly, the venue for the ceremony in few days, he was curious to find out the stance of new Korean government and the interests of the Korean business on the Trans-Pacific Partnership (TPP) from someone who is leading a think tank: Then, I was the President of the Korea Economic Research Institute (KERI).

The Canadian visitor knew that the Korean government was pursuing a Free Trade1 Agreement (FTA) with China, and China was upset about the TPP as the US conspiracy to contain China. His guess was that Korea would be in difficult position to join the TPP due to China. To the eyes of the outsiders, Seoul was in the orbit of Beijing. History proved that his guess was right. When the TPP talks were concluded in October 2015, Korea was not there, while Japan was on board. While joining the TPP seems to better serve the national interest of Korea, the government did not decide, perhaps could not, to join the TPP.

Two years later, in March 2015, Korea decided to join the China-led new international development bank in the name of the Asia Infrastructure Investment Bank (AIIB) as a founding member. The decision was done despite all those pressures from the US not to join. Does this confirm the perception of Seoul in the orbit of Beijing? As it turns out, starting with the UK, all the major European countries flocked to join the AIIB as the founding members. China intended to challenge the Western-led global economic governance.

When President Park Geun-hye stood along with President Xi Jinping at the Tiananmen Gate on September 3, 2015 for the military parade commemorating the 70th anniversary of the end of the World War II, she was the only head of the state from advanced industrial democracies. Her presence was interpreted as the strong state of the Korea-China relations. Few months later, the bilateral relations took the complete opposite direction and turned sour. Beijing became furious about Seoul's decision to deploy anti-missile system known as THAAD, and returned with severe and relentless trade retaliation. Ever-intensifying economic integration, common endeavors to create preferential trade agreement, and accumulated good will between Korea and China were not good enough to stop China's trade retaliation.

These unfolding events served a wake-up call to remind the very fragile nature of institutional arrangement on which Northeast Asia stands for its trade and investment. Being one of the most vibrant and dynamic economic zone in the globe, however, the three countries in Northeast Asia do not have preferential trading agreement among them. The China-Japan-Korea FTA talks were launched some year ago, but the progress has been between stop and slow. In the meantime, China has decided to turn itself into a self-sufficient technological powerhouse. So-called "Made in China 2025" blueprint was unveiled in 2015. In the process of implementing this ambitious blue print, China would turn upside down the global value chain of Northeast Asia. Implications for Korea, Japan and also the US would be far reaching and consequential. The future of trade and investment in Northeast Asia would not be the same as before. What sort of the future? My journey for the answer began.

During the past several years, the rise of China and the mega FTA were the two most popular subjects for conferences, seminars and workshops. What are challenges and opportunities from the rise of China? What are the future trajectories of mega FTA in Northeast Asia? In fact, these two questions are related to each other. I found out that discussions had subtle differences in nuances and connotations, varying by the national origins of experts. Japanese colleagues were more concerned about the assertive China, while my Chinese counterparts implied that it was not the rise of China to a unknown place, but the return of China to its historic place under the sun. All the American scholars I encountered wondered why Korea, as a major trading nation, did not join the TPP. They were puzzled why Korea was hesitant in making a natural step. Whenever I was compelled to offer my analysis, I found myself offering my views from the two different vintage points: as a Korean and also as a scholar. Time was always short for those responses. Hence, this book was conceived.

This book was begun in the summer of 2015 as a part of the book series from the Asiatic Research Institute of Korea University. A year later, a series of seismic events erupted. The U.K.'s decision to leave the EU (Brexit). The election of Trump. Candle light vigil in Korea, which eventually led to the impeachment of President Park. As a result, the book writing had to be back to the drawing board. I had to come up with a new approach and different cut of the political economic landscape of Northeast Asia. Reflections on these shattering moments suggested the new jargon of "New Normal" for a deeper understanding of what has been happening, and what are waiting to happen.

In this book, I offered my prognosis of Northeast Asia by 2030. In the intellectual circle of China, they were saying: "In 1949, only Communism could save China. In 1979, only Capitalism could China. In 1989, only China could save Communism. In 2009, only China could save Capitalism." What the future holds for China? The world is holding the breath. This book is an attempt to project trajectories for China's trade relations with the world.

At the time of completing this book, the US-China trade war has just erupted. After a year of preparation, Trump decided to impose prohibitive tariffs on $50 billion worth of the Chinese products and Xi reciprocated tit for tat. That the two largest trading nations and two biggest economies exchanged tariff bombs in such a massive scale is unprecedented in modern history. This may be only the beginning, however. Trump vowed to double down tariff imposition. If the second tariff bombing does happen, how will Xi respond?

The unfolding US-China trade war is a proxy fight for power struggle between the ruling power and the rising power. Trump vows to make

America great again, while Xi has publicly committed to make China great again. Trade war between the two largest economies would affect both Korea and Japan directly and indirectly. Trump is by any measure unconventional, and does not play with the conventional wisdom and the existing rule book. In his trade crusade, all the allies, including Korea and Japan, were rendered harsh unilateral treatment and are at loss what to do. Xi is no less determined to accomplish the Chinese Dream. He has already shown his appetite of resorting to geoeconomics to accomplish his goals. Whither the Northeast Asia? No one has a crystal ball for the future. Hope is that this book would give the reader some perspectives to better understand the undercurrents of "New Normal", the national interests of sovereign states with high stakes in Northeast Asia, and the grand strategies to navigate the turbulent sea of "New Normal." Welcome to the New Normal in Northeast Asia!

Acknowledgments

This book is an outgrowth of years of reflection on the future course of Northeast Asia's trade architecture. At every step of my journey from the very inception of envisaging a book like this to the writing of this book, so many people have inspired me, guided me, taught me, and helped me.

For trade strategies, I have been enjoying years of professional companionship with the most superb trade experts. When the Korean government decided to negotiate Free Trade Agreement with the US (known as "KORUS") in 2006, I took the initiative of organizing a group of scholars to exchange views and share thoughts on a regular basis. The group, named as 'Professors for Free Trade', was launched in the spring of 2006 and has grown to the focal point of discussing trade strategies among scholars and government officials. I vividly remember all those fierce and heated discussion on thorny issues of the KORUS, renegotiations, and ratification. The decision toward Korea's launching FTA with China, Trans Pacific Partnership were also debated seriously in the group. Years of intellectual exchanges with Heo Yoon, Choi Won-Mog, Chung Chul, Chung Inkyo, Ahn Dukgeun, Bark Taeho, and Ahn Se Young have led me to better understand deep structural challenges and come up with diverse and creative options.

Some bold strategic suggestions offered in this book date back to my days of the Korea Economic Research Institute as the President. Kim Chungsoo, Byun Yanggyu and Lee Kyounghee have joined my strategic initiatives of Service Big Bang, and Inclusive Trade Entrepreneurship. Looking back, those were great moments of thinking unthinkable. During those years, in collaboration with the Asian Development Bank (ADB), Factory Asia project was conceived. Rhee Changyong, then the Chief Economist of the ADB, now at the IMF, was instrumental in embarking on the project. The very idea of Factory China, which occupies a central conceptual framework of global value chain in Northeast Asia, has its genesis from this project.

For my perspectives on Japan and China, I have been lucky enough to be associated with the sharp mind and astute observers. Since 2008 I have been a regular participant to the Shanghai Forum and the Beijing Forum. Through these Forums, I have developed a long-lasting companionship with Chung Jae Ho, Jeong Jong-Ho, and Park Sung Joon. They have been my insatiable source of going deeper for any subject of China. Jae Ho's perspective on the hegemonic power struggle elevated my perspective on the US-China rivalry beyond trade and economy. Jong-Ho was the first person to teach me the significance of demographic dynamics of China. Sung Joon shared with me endless episodes of Chinese diplomacy which he witnessed and covered as a reporter from the early days of China's grand opening to the world.

Regarding trade policy of Japan, this book draws on my previous and on-going research with my coauthor, Jennifer Oh. I am also grateful to Park Cheol-Hee for his insight on Japan. The Korea-Japan Strategic Dialogue, which he organized in June 2016, brought me home the concerns of the

Japanese about the assertive China. Choi Seokyoung, the former chief trade negotiator for the KORUS and the former Korean ambassador to Geneva, has been willing to share with me complication and subtlety of trade policy making from the front line. His generosity for time and candid discussion are much appreciated.

During the academic years of 2014-2016, I have offered my experimental course on Political Economy of East Asia. The course was designed to look back the past 100 years of conflict in Northeast Asia and look forward the years to 2050 for Northeast Asia. Students were assigned to their thought experiment of scenario building for the future trajectories of Northeast Asia. In the class, I have challenged student with the questions of "what if." The innocence and wild imagination of my students constantly inspired me to look for a reasoned way out.

My special thanks go to the Trilateral Cooperation Secretariat (TCS), and the Korea International Trade Association (KITA). They were generous enough to offer me privilege of keynote addresses and moderating at several high-profile international conferences. Those occasions provided time for reflection on the current status and the future of trade and investment in Northeast Asia. I am grateful for Lee Jong-heon, Secretary General of the TCS, and Sakong Il, Han Duck Soo, and Kim In Ho, the former Chairmen of the KITA for their generosity.

The Korea Foundation for Advanced Studies (KFAS) deserves special mention in shaping my perspective on China. The Shanghai Forum, the Beijing Forum, and other Forum organized by the KFAS have provided me with invaluable venues to meet with sharp-minded scholars. Park In-kook, the President of KFAS, pioneered to launch "Understanding China" lecture series and Trilateral Conference among Korea, China and the US. I had privilege of giving a talk at the Understanding China. The occasion propelled my intellectual quest for the future of China and its relations with major trading nations. I have been partaking in the Trilateral Conference from its inception in 2014. So far, the six rounds of events took places. Every round has seen intense debates and spirited exchanges. North Korea's acceleration of nuclear path, paramount changes in China and the new developments of the US-China relations have fueled the debate. From these processes, I became increasingly aware of unique Chinese perspective on history and international relations. Jia Qingguo, Zhang Yunling, and Zhu Fung, among others, have unashamedly offered their views to my straightforward and often provocative questions.

From the idea to the publication of this book was not possible without the support of Lee Jong-Wha, Director of Asiatic Research Institute, Korea University. During the protracted and painful process of writing, I was fortunate enough to get valuable assistance from Kim Eunhae, Joo Bora, and Jang Jiwon.

I thank my family for their moral support and encouragement. Ji Young has been patient and understanding of my dire plight of meeting the deadline of the manuscript. Her encouragement meant a lot, as my winter night was extended to another dawn in the next day. This book is dedicated to the memory of my father and my father-in-law. They were born and spent their childhood in the colonial period. As the newborn citizens of a newly independent country, they worked tirelessly to overcome hunger and poverty. Their struggle is now recorded as a miracle, which transformed the poorest nation in the world to an affluent nation with its place in the global map. Without their blood and tears, my generation would not have enjoyed this much of political liberty and economic freedom. Without their valor and undefeated optimism against all odds, I would not have attained this high commanding post to ponder on the future of Northeast Asia.

1 Northeast Asia at Crossroads

In the snow wonderland of a small Swiss town, the most powerful man from China took the podium in front of a jam-packed audience. It was on January 17, 2017, during the annual gathering of the prominent and influential from all over the globe. At the World Economic Forum, better known as the Davos Forum, President Xi Jinping from China had something to say:

> *"There was a time when China also had doubts about economic globalization, and was not sure whether it should join the World Trade Organization. But we came to the conclusion that integration into the global economy is a historical trend. To grow its economy, China must have the courage to swim in the vast ocean of the global market. If one is always afraid of bracing the storm and exploring the new world, he will sooner or later get drowned in the ocean. Therefore, China took a brave step to embrace the global market. We have had our fair share of choking in the water and encountered whirlpools and choppy waves, but we have learned how to swim in this process. It has proved to be a right strategic choice.*

Whether you like it or not, the global economy is the big ocean that you cannot escape from. Any attempt to cut off the flow of capital, technologies, products, industries and people between economies, and channel the waters in the ocean back into isolated lakes and creeks is simply not possible. Indeed, it runs counter to the historical trend."

The Chinese economy has grown so rapidly since the historic "reform and opening" year of 1978. Coming into the new millennium, China continued to grow rapidly. In 2011 China overtook Japan to become the second largest economy, a title Japan had owned for more than four decades. The world began to debate when China would overtake the US and become the largest economy in the world. The International Monetary Fund (IMF) announced in 2014 that in terms of purchasing power parity (PPP), China became the largest economy in the world, putting the US in second place for the first time in 142 years. The meteoric rise of China is arguably the single most significant event in modern history. China's phenomenal growth has lifted over 700 million people out of poverty, and dramatically enhanced the living standards of 1.3 billion Chinese people. China's entry into the World Trade Organization (WTO) has proved instrumental in the economic miracle of China.

China is no longer the world factory of cheap consumer products. Mobile economy is transforming the landscape of the Chinese economy. Alibaba, Tencent, and Baidu, the top three internet companies in China, are compared to Amazon, Facebook, and Google of the US. The market value of Tencent, Chinese internet giant, is bigger than that of Facebook. DiDi Chuxing, a local ride-sharing company, became the most valuable start-up company in the world in 2017. The mobile economy of China is assessed to be the biggest market in the world, and its speed of growth is just spectacular.

The story of Shenzhen is a vivid display of the rise of China, and of its far-reaching impact on the global economy. China chose Shenzhen as its first special economic zone to pilot China's opening up to overseas investors. Within the time span of 30 years, Shenzhen has transformed from a small fishing village to the world capital of electronics and information technology (IT), placing itself on the global map. Yet the story of Shenzhen is far from over. Shenzhen has an ambition to become a world leader in innovation as well as the center of "Designed in China." The ambition is rapidly turning into a reality. Most of the world's drones are made in Shenzhen. Airbus recently announced Shenzhen as the location for its China innovation center.

When Xi was speaking highly of globalization in Davos, he had one person in mind: Donald Trump. Trump, in his first week as new President of the US, withdrew his country from the Trans-Pacific Partnership (TPP), the biggest trade agreement ever, just few days prior to Xi's moment in Davos. The TPP, a 12-nation trade agreement among the US, Japan, Mexico, Canada, Australia, New Zealand, Vietnam, Peru, Chile, Malaysia, Singapore, and Brunei, was negotiated under former U.S. President Barack Obama. The TPP was signed in February 2016, and was waiting for its ratification before entry into force. However, the US failed to ratify the TPP in the final year of Obama as President. Incoming President Trump took the US out of the TPP. The exclusion of the US from the 12-states Pacific-Rim pact would mean that eight years of negotiations over 32 rounds now comes to ground zero. The decision to pull the US out of the TPP was a major disaster for the 11 other signatories. Trump's move signaled the beginning of the end of the world where the US was leading the liberal international economic order. The departure of the US from the TPP meant that the US would retreat from the driver seat of globalization. Welcome to the brave new world of "Globalization without America!" Globalization without American would imply a great deal of uncertainty about the future of the American influence in Asia and in the world. The limelight was now on China.

While Xi, as the top leader of the second-largest economy with a striking distance of overtaking the US, was assuring the world that China would not retreat from the challenges of globalization, something to the contrary of his remarks was taking place. A number of Korean products and services, better known as K-cosmetics, K-pop, and K-surgery, were the target of boycott in China. As a reaction to the deployment of the US-developed anti-ballistic missile system known as Terminal High Altitude Area Defense (THAAD) in the soil of South Korea, which was designed as a defense against nuclear attack from North Korea, China has launched a kind of shadow boycott of almost all Korean things.

Lotte, a Korean company, which offered a location for the installation of THAAD, became the public enemy of the Chinese. Its Chinese branches faced angry demonstration and retaliation. Months of boycott drove out customers. Lotte department stores in China became ghost house. The deteriorating business environment forced the company to find abrupt exit from China. Entertainment performances of Korean celebrities in China were cancelled one after another. All these were related to THAAD. Severe damage was felt in Korea's tourism sector. In protest against Seoul's decision to deploy THAAD, Chinese travel agencies prohibited selling package tours going to Korea. All the Chinese group tours into Korea came to a sudden and complete halt. Jeju, a major tourist destination for Chinese tourists, has been hit the hardest. The island has since turned into a town of silence.

What is wrong with THHAD in Korea? In the wake of escalating North Korean nuclear provocations, the Koran government approved the deployment of THAAD in 2016 as a defensive measure. Beijing argued that THAAD could be used to spy on its own missile program. As for the Korean government, the deployment of THAAD was a crucial element of its security defense. Chinese opposition was irksome, but could not change the course of action. For Beijing, THAAD was a US-China issue, not a South Korea-North Korea issue. Any consideration for Seoul's increasing security concern did not have any place in the strategic map of Beijing. Hence, Korea's largest trading partner turned to trade retaliation to put pressure on Korea. Beijing embarked on virtual economic sanctions. Sales of Korean restaurants in the Beijing area have plunged by a third year-on-year. Sales of Hyundai and Kia Motors have fallen by half. Many small and medium-sized Korean businesses in China left the country.

China is Korea's largest trading partner. A quarter of Korea's annual trade is with China. Korean investment, products, and technology have been instrumental in the rise of China. Since the normalization of diplomatic relations in 1992, the two countries never had a dispute of this magnitude. President Moon Jae-in, the new leader of Korea who came to power through the candle-light vigil during the impeachment of then-President Park Geun-hye, had a priority in resolving on-going THAAD-related economic retaliation. Instead of confronting the angry and resentful Chinese government head-to-head, he was turning to low-key diplomacy. In his speech at Peiking University in December 2017 on the margin of his summit with Xi Jinping, Moon said:

> *China truly shines when it harmonizes with its surrounding nations, not when it stands alone. It is like how high mountain peaks get higher as it harmonizes with the many surrounding peaks. In that sense, I hope China's dream is not just China's but a dream shared by all of Asia, and ven the entire humanity.*
>
> *There are two assignments that humanity has still failed to solve. The first is permanent peace and the second is common prosperity. I believe these will become feasible dreams when China further embraces diversity and unfolds its spirit of openness and tolerance. Albeit a small country, Korea, as a responsible middle power state, shall join the Chinese dream.*

Korea and China entered into a Free Trade Agreement (Korea-China FTA) in 2015. It was China's first FTA with a major manufacturing economy. The scope and depth of trade liberalization commitment in Korea-China FTA was not up to the expectations of the Korean business sector, while service and investment issues were not even seriously negotiated. In order to rectify this problem, China agreed to the second stage negotiations on service and investment issues after two years of entry into force. As of December 2017, the time has arrived. This second-stage negotiation is critical for Korea. When Seoul was first negotiating with Beijing for FTA, it strongly demanded the opening-up of service and investment in China. Beijing was not ready for it. Stalemate continued. The fate of FTA was hung in the air. Without Beijing's forward-looking concession, negotiations were in impasse. Political consideration on the part of Seoul inched toward a compromise with Beijing's offer of second stage negotiations on service and investment. In the margin of the Beijing APEC Leaders' Summit in November 2014, top leaders of Korea and China announced that they got the deal. In retrospect, 2014 was the peak of the Korea-China honeymoon.

History turned its interesting corner. When Beijing embarked on shadow trade retaliation due to THAAD deployment, the Korea-China FTA proved of little usage. Against this changing tide, the prevailing sentiment in Seoul was pessimistic about the second stage negotiations. Even under good relations, the second stage negotiations on service and investment seemed to be tough and rocky. Whither the Korea-China FTA? Whither the Korea-China trade relations?

As Moon was delivering his remarks to the young Chinese, Korea trade officials were busy back in Seoul with their preparation of upcoming negotiations for amending the Korea-US Free Trade Agreement (KORUS FTA). The KORUS FTA was in its fifth year of implementation. The

KORUS FTA was regarded as a critical pillar of the Korea-US alliance, cementing the existing Korea-US security alliance. For the long and winding journey to the KORUS FTA from its inception, both Korean and American sides committed politically to the successful completion of the KORUS FTA against the all odds and obstacles. The Korean leadership had to confront strong anti-American sentiments and fierce opposition from import-competing sectors, championed by the farming sector. The American leadership had to deal with its auto industry, which forged alliance with sympathetic politicians, calling the KORUS FTA 'unfair.' Since 2012, the first year of entry into force, the KORUS FTA was regarded a model case of mutually beneficial trade agreement. However, the election of President Trump, who lambasted all major US trade deals as 'horrible' and 'job-killing,' had consequences to the KORUS FTA. Due to Trump's threat to terminate the agreement, the Korean government was forced to sit down with its American counterpart to revisit the KORUS FTA. The US publicized the imbalance in the auto trade as a major factor for widening trade deficit vis-à-vis Korea. Wither the KORUS FTA? Wither the Korea-US trade relations?

From the other side of the planet, another noteworthy development was unfolding in the same month of December. The WTO biennial Ministerial Conference was taking place in Buenos Aires, Argentina. It was the 11th Ministerial since the establishment of the WTO in 1995. The WTO Ministerial is supposed to conclude with the adoption of Joint Declaration. Even though the WTO was in deep trouble, as evidenced by its inability to wrap up the longest-running trade negotiations in history under the name of Doha Development Agenda (DDA), launched in 2001, the tradition would be kept, according to conventional wisdom. Trade officials would fight for and against languages in the draft document before the Ministerial. At the previous Ministerial, the US expressed its frustration with the modus operandi of existing multilateral negotiations, and called for a new approach to DDA. At the 2015 WTO Ministerial in Nairobi, Kenya, US Trade Representative Froman said: "Doha issues are too important to leave to the Doha architecture that has failed for so long."[1]

This time was different. The Buenos Aires WTO Ministerial ended without Joint Declaration. For the first time in the WTO history, Ministers failed to adopt Joint Declaration. The bone of contention was "free and open" trade versus "reciprocal and fair" trade. Robert Lighthizer, the US Trade Representative was openly critical of the WTO, in particular of the dispute settlement system - perhaps the most imortant feature of the WTO:

> *"The WTO is losing its essential focus on negotiation and becoming a litigation-centered organization. Too often members seem to believe they can gain concessions through lawsuits that they could never get at the negotiating table. We have to ask ourselves whether this is good for the institution and whether the current litigation structure makes sense."*[2]

1 Michael Froman (2015).

2 Opening Plenary Statement of USTR Robert Lighthizer at the WTO Ministerial Conference 2017.

The US looks determined to pursue a unilateral approach. Lighthizer also stated:

> "*Many members recognized that the WTO must pursue a fresh start in key areas so that like-minded WTO Members and their constituents are not held back by the few Members that are not ready to act. In this regard, the United States is pleased to work with willing Members on e-commerce, scientific standards for agricultural products, and the challenges of unfair trade practices that distort world markets." (emphasis added)*[3]

The WTO, the mainstay of the global trading system, is being discredited by its architect and its largest stakeholder, the US. The US trade policy under President Trump turned to reciprocity and bilateralism, while it discarded multilateralism. Moreover, it began to measure the balance of bilateral trade as the most important yardstick of trade policy.

The break-up of the TPP by the US hit Japan hardest. Prime Minister Abe Shinzo's economic blueprint for Japan met an unexpected obstacle. His blueprint, so-called Abenomics, had three "arrows" of key policy measures. Using the TPP as external pressure to reform Japan's stifling regulatory system with the aim of enhancing productivity was one of these arrows. The TPP is the biggest free trade agreement Japan has ever joined. Top leaders

3 Statement of USTR Lighthizer at the conclusion of the WTO Ministerial Conference 2017.

of Japan and the US, Abe and Obama, worked hard to bring the TPP talks into fruition. The TPP was called as the US-Japan alliance, not only for its economic significance but also for its strategic alliance against the rise of assertive China. During the whole process of pushing the TPP, Obama claimed that the TPP was about writing the trading rule of the 21st century, and that the US would not allow China to write the rule. The TPP was, to the eyes of many, the Obama administration's pinnacle of the Rebalancing to Asia strategy. Such strategic imperative of the US met with Abe's economic revitalization strategy for Japan.

Then, does the US departure from the TPP imply that the US would be less interested in forging economic and strategic coalition with Japan against China? Does the US withdrawal from the TPP imply that the US would be less interested in confronting and containing China? In the light of campaign records and track records since the start of Trump's presidency, the US-China trade confrontation will be inevitable. Trump is serious about reducing huge trade deficits vis-à-vis China and rectifying unfair trade. Experts wonder why Trump does not use perhaps the most effective trade strategy to contain China. Prior to Trump, the US had a concerted and coordinated approach in dealing with China in the sphere of trade. Negotiating FTA with Korea and then the TPP along with Japan were exemplary acts. While the rise of China continues, and China becomes increasingly assertive in projecting its power and articulating its interests, the US under the Trump threatens to terminate the KORUS FTA and pulled the US out of the TPP, shaking US-Japan economic alliance against Japan.

Taken all these developments together, the Northeast Asia is at a crossroads. The previous road, which has taken the region to prosperity, affluence, and peace since the end of the Cold War, is about to reach its end. Korea, Japan, and China have been riding the high tide of globalization spearheaded by the US. Now, the US seems less interested in maintaining the very trading system it pioneered, expanded, and strengthened. For the remarkable success story of Northeast Asia, the access to the biggest market in the world, the US, and the political commitment to the global trading system, which was also assured by the US, were instrumental. Now, those are about to disappear.

Most significantly, the US-China relations would not be the same. But for the US engagement policy of China, China's place in the WTO would not have been possible. Without its membership at the WTO, the story of China so far would have been rather different. Washington's presumption of engaging with China has been guided by the belief that engagement would lead to more liberal China through economic development. What has taken place in China is not up to such belief. To the dismay of Washington, the bigger and prosperous China did not change its political system. Since the reign of Xi Jinping, Beijing intensified its political repression and consolidated the power of the Communist Party. With ever-strong political control, Beijing's promise of reform and opening up further has been largely on document. Under the politically repressed regime, China for now is economically powerful with less willingness to open up more to the outside world. Such a combination of economy and politics inevitably gives rise to increasing risks of doing business in China.

With its super-sized domestic economy, Beijing has turned harsh on foreign investors. Episodes of discrimination and mandatory technology transfer are piling up. Opaque regulatory system and no arm's length relations between the government and the Communist Party add the seriousness of hidden and unexpected risks. How to protect foreign investors from these inherent risks? On the other hand, whilst not opening up its market further, China is getting aggressive in going abroad. China aims to acquire foreign assets, skills, and technologies through cross-border mergers and acquisitions (M&A). Deep pocket of the Chinese investors in the global market has already raised eyebrows in Washington and many Capitals of the Western countries. From the outsider's point of view, the key question is how to address this asymmetry of market access. From Beijing's point of view, the question is how far can it advance without changing its political economic system?

The new US under Trump has adopted the mantra of reciprocal and fair trade. Reciprocity may be defined in many different ways. Fairness also defies a single measurement. Who would define reciprocity and fairness? How much reciprocity and fairness would be required? One question leads to another. It appears that the US alone decides all the answers to such questions. All in all, the headwind of reciprocal and fair trade from Washington will turn global trade upside down. Global trading system is under the growing threat of moving from rule-based multilateral system to power-based bilateral system. International economic architecture is witnessing the end of liberal international order. With Washington turning inside and Beijing becoming increasingly assertive, Korea and Japan find themselves losing a staunch balancer in the region. Whither Northeast Asia?

Questions for the Future

This book is an attempt to project possible future trajectories of economic architecture of Northeast Asia by 2030. Why 2030? A number of simulations have projected that by then China would have become or about to be the largest economy in the world, overtaking the US. If the US grows annually 2.5% and China by 6%, for instance, China will become the largest economy in 2026. Either higher Chinese growth or lower the US growth compared to this benchmark will fasten the time for trading places. In terms of PPP (purchasing power parity), according to the IMF, China has already become the largest economy in the world in 2014. Some scholars point out the possibility of China caught in middle-income trap, or major economic crisis in China.[4] In either case, trading places would not take place by 2030 at the least. Even though taking places between China and the US may not

---

4 Middle-income trap refers to a situation where a country, reaching at a middle income status due to rapid growth, finds itself incapable of further catching up with high-income countries. There has been rising concern that China may fall into such a trap. For instance, Glawe and Wagner (2017) argue that China should implement reforms to avoid middle-income trap. The analysis of Huang and et al (2017) argues that China faces the risk of middle-income trap because of declining industrial share and growth rate of productivity.

happen by 2030, rapidly closing gap between the two great powers would make more of confrontation and conflicts, and less of cooperation as business as usual.[5]

As 〈Table 1〉 demonstrates, China becomes increasingly assertive over the time. In particular, in security and territorial issues China becomes more vocal, non-compromising, and going-it-alone. As evidenced in the case of the South China Sea, Senkaku/Diaoyu dispute, and trade retaliation in relation to the THAAD, this aspect of rise of assertive China poses serious challenges to Korea and Japan. What was foreseen at the turn of century has become a major question for Northeast Asia now: "The rise of a new power has been attended by uncertainty and anxieties. Often, though not always, violent conflict has followed. The rise in the economic and military power of China, the world's most populous country, will be a central question for Asia and for American foreign policy at the beginning of a new century."[6]

By 2030 China will have had time for implementing its blueprint for transforming China from the global factory to the global consumer, from investment-driven to consumption-driven, and from quantity to quality. China's success in 'Made in China 2025' would have been determined by then.

---

5 When an emerging power challenges the existing power, history shows, more often than not, the power transition has not been peaceful. The most recent power transition between the Great Britain and the US, which was less confrontational, is regarded as exception. Alison (2013) and Mearsheimer (2013) assert that a possibility of forthcoming war between the US and China.

6 Nye (1999)

China's Belt Road Initiative (BRI) will have been implemented to some extent, with various consequences, along with its Asian Infrastructure Investment Bank (AIIB) in action. On-going technological breakthrough of digital economy, known as the 4th Industrial Revolution of Digital Transformation, provides golden opportunity for China to leapfrog and achieve the status of technologically advanced country.

Effectiveness and speed of China's transformation will be played on the strategic canvass of Northeast Asia. In projecting future trajectories of economic architecture of Northeast Asia by 2030, two strategic games need close scrutiny. One is the contest between China, the rising power, and the US, the incumbent power. As the global power, the US will try to contain the US in the region so that China will find itself more difficult to project its power on other spheres of the globe. As an aspiring regional power, China will have to confront the US containment strategy. The contest between China and its neighbor countries (Korea and Japan) is another strategic game. Korea and Japan have been integral part of the Global Value Chain (GVC) in the region with China as the assembly forefront. Economic relationship among Korea, Japan and China has been characterized more of cooperation than less of competition in the sense that they needed each other in the effective operation of GVC in the region. Transformation of China in coming years would challenge the sustainability of this division of production network in the region.

While conflicts in Northeast Asia on the rise with the rise of assertive China, case for further economic engagement has not receded. Being inspired by the success of the European common market, and North America through a series of regional trade agreements aiming for freer and intensified flow of products, services, money, people, and idea, the vision of Northeast Asia economic integration is still out there to fulfill. While Europe and North American achieved a high level of economic common interface among countries, Northeast Asia has a long way to go. At the present, there is no regional trade agreement covering all countries in Northeast Asia. Even though they launched trilateral FTA talks, so far progress has been slow. In this context, the future of Northeast Asia will be contested among nationalism, populism, and globalism.

With China attempting to transform itself from quantity to quality, how much common interface will it attempt to create with the US and its neighbors, Korea and Japan? This is the main question of this book. In order to come up with realistic futures, this book will adopt the two-level game perspective as a research framework and also for the narrative.[7] Two-level in the sense that interaction between domestic level and international level, and between political hyper-structure and economic infrastructure is analyzed. In the two-level setup, how nationalism, populism, and globalism shape debates and influence stakeholders in the geopolitical political sphere of Northeast Asia will be explored.

So far, a substantial amount of research has been made in the broad

7 The concept of two-level game is first used by Putnam (1988).

theme of Northeast Asia economic integration. Existing works in East Asian economic integrations are overdosed on economics, while political dimension is sidelined. Various options of integration from loosely-defined economic cooperation to more-tightly integrated community based on international negotiations and treaty have been studied. While these works demonstrated theoretical possibilities for the Northeast Asian economic integration, most of these works are normative, driven by the urge to conclude that more integration would be beneficial. Arguing for the beneficial side of economic integration, but short on the cost and the losers risks the danger of painting a rosy picture, detached from the real world. The existing literature pays scant attention to political realities of Northeast Asia, where nationalism and populism run rampant, standing in the way of forging ahead toward any deeper economic integration. For instance, a collection of papers in Chun and Park (2011) on the theme of Northeast Asia integration displays this bias. In this book, political economy of Korea, Japan and China will be given a closer look to identify obstacles and challenges, idiosyncratic factors and common challenges. As framework for studying Northeast Asia economic integration, Ahn and Park (2007) emphasized the importance of incorporating domestic political institutions, but they did not have strategic contest between the US and China as crucial element. Without deep understanding of the US-China rivalry, the future trajectory of Northeast Asia will not be explored.

Roadmap of the book

The analytical framework of the book is to be laid out in Chapter 2, taking the case of Factory China. Factory China is analytical framework and also metaphor for GVC established in Northeast Asia. For Factory China to be operational and lead Northeast Asia to its remarkable economic achievement, linkage among ideology, institution, and technology was critical. Ideology of free and open trade, multilateral institution, and integrative technology reinforced each other and gave rise to so-called liberal international order. Emergence of Factory China and continuing stellar economic performance of Northeast Asia owe a lot to this nexus. China's accession to the WTO was instrumental for the success of Factory China. Without ideology of trade promoting peace and security, China's seat at the WTO would not have been possible. In addition, technology of Information and Communication was also critical to establish globally expanded and connected production network. Chapter 2 identifies the nexus among these three factors and sets up the baseline framework for the book.

Institutional underpinning of Factory China is one-dimension, compared to other GVCs such as North American Free Trade Area (NAFTA) and European Union (EU). Mindful of this gap, Northeast Asian countries have tried to strengthen institutional foundation of the nexus. What has happened in the region of Northeast Asia since the dawn of the new millennium can be labelled as "economic architecture contest" or "contest toward deep integration". As it turns out, the contest has not always been under common grand design among countries. It looks like journey without a map. Pathway for deep integration has not been linear. Sometimes, two steps forward were followed by two steps backward. It took much time for Korea, Japan and China to agree to move collectively forward the next stage of their economic integration. After spending the first decade of the new millennium in their individual trade preemptive move against the others, the three countries of Korea, Japan and China came to an agreement to launch their trilateral FTA. Whereas the journey began, travelers have no common sense of their final destination. Domestic political economic differences give rise to different preference for pathways and destinations. What has happened so far is the subject of Chapter 3 and 4.

In the first decade of the 21st century, countries in the Northeast Asia were mindful of creating their own strategic advantage through bilateral FTA. Korea's surprising and remarkable success is analyzed in Chapter 3, with contrast of stagnant Japan and China. The watershed was Korea's decision to negotiate with the US for the bilateral FTA (KORUS). It was Korea, not the US, which requested negotiations for the KORUS. More remarkably, it was the left-leaning government elected on the wave of anti-American populism.

Coming into the second decade of the new millennium, countries are beginning to move into regional and mega-regional FTA. The limelight was on the contest between the US and China. Being aware of the rise of China, the US decided to deploy "Rebalancing to Asia". The TPP has become the US strategic tool to advance its interests in the region. Japan, under the renewed political leadership, found its economic and strategic interest in joining the TPP. Korea decided not to join the TPP. Instead, it pursued bilateral FTA with China, which was also outside of the TPP. As counterstrategy to the TPP, China came up with its own initiatives, including BRI. TPP negotiations among 12 Asia Pacific countries came to a successful conclusion. However, Trump, the new President of the US, took the US out of the TPP. Chapter 4 analyzes the evolution of the TPP and changing political economy.

Historical account of Chapter 3 and 4 serves background for the main question of this book: projecting the trajectories of Northeast Asia to 2030. For an effective projection, one needs to understand the deep change of exiting Ideology-Institution-Technology Nexus in Northeast Asia. Chapter 5 describes the newly emerging Ideology-Institution-Technology Nexus in the region. "New Normal" is short-hand for this new nexus. Main features of the New Normal and the reasons behind its emergence are analyzed. In Chapter 6, domestic political economic landscape of China, Korea, and Japan is analyzed. Here, focus is on changing ideological landscape in Northeast Asia. How much impact of New Normal is being felt in each country in the region will be analyzed. We will argue the decline globalism in contrast with the rise of nationalism and populism in the region, with far-reaching implication for future trajectory of economic integration in Northeast Asia. Common external factors facing Northeast Asia - rapid aging and digital transformation - are also discussed in Chapter 6. Domestic political economy plays as constraints, while common external factors may be utilized as opportunities for creating interface among nations. Chapter

6 will discuss the US-China strategic game, with the analysis of drivers, conflict zones, and interests of each side.

Building on analysis of Chapter 5 and 6, several scenarios for the future trajectories to 2030 are presented in Chapter 7. Several scenarios are to be imagined. Reality check and strategic analysis of each scenario will be attempted. In selecting plausible scenario, differences in approach to deep integration by China and the US will be highlighted and analyzed. The book concludes by offering a more desirable, yet possible and plausible picture of future economic architecture in Northeast Asia.

Table 1 Milestones in Northeast Asia

2008	The outbreak of the Global Financial Crisis G20 created as ad hoc global economic steering group, replacing G7 The first G20 Summit in Washington, DC (November 16-17, 2008)
2010	Seoul hosts the G20 summit (2010 G20 Seoul summit: November 11-12, 2010)
2011	The Korea-US FTA ratified, while the opposition in Korea was strong (The U.S. ratified the treaty on October 12, 2011. South Korea ratified it on November 22, 2011)
2012	The Korea-US FTA entered into force on March 15, 2012 Xi Jinping becomes the new leader of China (assumed office on November 15, 2012) Abe becomes the prime minister of Japan (assumed office on December 26, 2012) Park Geun-hye elected as the president of Korea (elected on December 19, 2012; assumed office on February 25, 2013)
2013	Abe unveils the economic revitalization of Japan, known as the Abenomics Japan decides to join the TPP talks (March 2013) China, Japan, Korea begin to negotiate the trilateral FTA among them (CJK FTA) Xi pledges economic reform at the 3rd Plenum (November 2013) China unveils the One Belt One Road(OBOR) initiative (The Silk Road Economic Belt concept was introduced on September 2013; The Belt and Road initiative was mentioned again on November 2013, at the Third Plenary Session.) China proposes the idea of Asian Infrastructure Investment Bank (AIIB) (October 2013)

2014	Beijing hosts the APEC Summit (November 10-12, 2014), and the US and China are at odds with the FTAAP (Free Trade Area of Asia Pacific) The completion of Korea-China FTA announced at the Beijing APEC Summit Abe proposes the amendment of the Constitution, changing Article 9 (Abe proposed a new constitutional interpretation of Article 9 on February 13, 2014.)
2015	AIIB created under the Chinese leadership. Korea joined the TPP, while Japan and the US did not join Korean President Park attends The 70th Anniversary of the Victory of the Chinese People's War of Resistance Against Japanese Aggression and The World Anti-Fascist War, while no one from the US and Japan attended (September 3, 2015) TPP agreed (October 2015). US president Obama claim: "TPP is about who writes trade rule for the 21st century. We cannot allow China to write it" THAAD installation in Korea, In China boycott of Korean products and services Korea-Japan agreement on the "comfort women" issue (December 28, 2015)
2016	China hosts G20 Summit (2016 G20 Hangzhou Summit: September 4-5, 2016) Donald Trump, promising "Make America great again", elected as the US President, based on aggressive anti-China rhetoric (elected on November 8, 2016; assumed office on January 20, 2017) "China is a currency manipulator" North Korea conducts its 4th and 5th nuclear test (January and September, respectively)
2017	The US withdraws from the TPP (January 2017), leaving the fate of the TPP at the hands of 11 states. The US begins the investigation of China IPR violation under Section 301 of the Trade Act of 1974 (August 2017) South Korean President Park Geun-hye ousted from power (The Constitutional Court upheld the impeachment on March 10, 2017) Moon Jae-in elected as new President of Korea (May 9, 2017) Moon orders to revisit the Korea-Japan agreement on "comfort women" (On December 2017, President Moon Jae-in says the 2015 agreement has serious flaws.) North Korea conducts its 6th nuclear test, the UN adopts sanction (September 2017) TPP 11 (without the US) agreed under the initiative of Japan (November 2017) Xi consolidates his power at the 19th Chinese Communist Party Congress, and declares the vision of the Chinese Dream (2050: the most rich and powerful nation) (October 2017)

2 Ideology-Institution-Technology Nexus in Northeast Asia

Korea, Japan, and China - three states in Northeast Asia - are members of G20 (Group 20), which began its life in the midst of the 2008 Global Economic Crisis. Prior to the 2008 Crisis, the G7 (Group of 7) had played the role of a global economic steering group, Japan being the only Asian state in G7. The 2008 Crisis, however, changed the global economic governance structure completely. A few months after the onset of the financial meltdown in Wall Street, the US called for an ad hoc Summit of 20 significantly important economies, instead of relying on the G7. The idea behind the G20 Summit was to bring on board the national leaders from the top ten advanced countries and the top ten emerging countries. Considering the economic power shift from the Western countries to the emerging ones, which was already taking place prior to the 2008 Crisis, the ineffectiveness and lack of credibility of the G7 became clear. Various proposals for something more inclusive than the G7 were suggested prior to the 2008 Crisis, but remained only at the table. When the financial crisis erupted in the US with the potential of bringing the world to the cliff of unprecedented economic crisis, President Bush did not hesitate to designate the new group of G20 and called for the G20 Summit in Washington, D.C. in the dire effort to stabilize the global market. Remarkably, all three countries in Northeast Asia joined the G20. There is no better way to demonstrate the economic significance of the three Northeast Asian states.

1. Northeast Asia and the Global Trading System

Korea, Japan, and China belong to the top 7 global trading economies. The three countries have pursued trade-oriented growth strategies. The three also promoted heavy and chemical industries. Over time, Japan, Korea, and China, one after another in sequence, have become global major powers in those sectors.

The remarkable economic success of Japan, Korea, and China cannot be separated from their linkage in the global trading system. Without steady expansion of trade, they could not have enjoyed a long period of sustained economic growth. Without effective integration to the global trading system, their trade performance would have been vulnerable to political and economic risks. All three countries expanded their trade under the GATT (General Agreement on Tariffs and Trade) / WTO system.[8]

---

8 The GATT played de facto international trade organization until 1994. The completion of the Uruguay Round gave a birth to the WTO (World Trade Organization), which began its life from January 1995. Hence, GATT/WTO is the expression for the multilateral global trading system.

Japan joined the GATT in 1955. Korea followed suit by acceding to the GATT in 1967. Lastly, China joined the WTO in 2001.[9] Unlike Japan and Korea, China's accession to the global trading system took quite a long time. China decided to join the GATT in 1986, and 15 years passed until China finally secure its seat in the WTO. The decision of Deng Xiaoping in 1978 to open up China for international trade was a historical moment. However, the steps taken by China were gradual, incremental, and cautious. Nonetheless, it was a grand and historic opening, because China did not look back and steadily pursued for more integration with the global trading system. In this regard, the decision to seek a membership at the GATT was momentous. The negotiation process put to test China's will to reform and open up. China knew that once in the GATT, it would be difficult to change its course of navigation.

To begin with, a membership at the GATT meant that China would be required to open up substantially. Not just tariffs but non-tariffs barriers of China w ould be subject to accession negotiations. The biggest pressure would come from the US, the biggest market China would gain for its non-discriminatory access. Of course, other members of the GATT would press hard on China for their priority list as well. To prepare for these

---

9 As a matter of fact, China was the original member of the GATT when it was launched in 1948 with 23 members. It was China led by the KMT(Nationalist), and China was in the civil war between the nationalist and the communist. The Chinese civil ended with the victory of the communist led by Mao in 1949. The KMT fled to Taiwan, and somehow it disappeared from the GATT.

negotiations, China should have its house in order first. Having spent so many years under virtual economic isolation, putting in place China's trade structure (tariffs and non-tariffs measures) was a tall order. Preparation for negotiations would be followed by negotiations between China and the GATT members

Secondly, China's membership at the GATT meant future market opening of China. The GATT had pursued progressive liberalization through a series of multilateral trade negotiations, known as the Round. When China was contemplating its accession for the GATT, the Tokyo Round of the 1970s was the latest negotiations under the aegis of the GATT, and the new Round - soon to be named as the Uruguay Round - was about to be launched. In case of prompt accession, China would take a part in this Round. In case of prolonged accession, China would be demanded to undertake parallel liberalization steps in line with the on-going trade Round.

Third, accession to the GATT meant that China would follow the dispute settlement procedure of the GATT. All the trade disputes involving China, either as a complaint or an accused, would be resolved pursuant to the rules set by others.

In short, China's accession to the global trading system meant that China accepted the global trading system set by the Western powers. China could not change the game rules, even though it did not agree with them. When China decided to switch its modus operandi of economy from isolation to opening up, the Cold War was at its peak. The liberal camp was championed by the US, and the communist side was led by the Soviet Union. In this context, China's decision to open up trade to the liberal camp was a sea change. However, opening up was one thing, and accession to the global trading system was another. Opening up was a political act, which may be reversible, while accession to the GATT/WTO would make such political act almost irreversible.[10]

It took 15 years for China to accede to the global trading system. Negotiations with the US were the toughest. The US was keenly aware that China would not be easy to handle once inside the system. Hence, the US did not want to miss the historic opportunity of opening up the Chinese market. What had also complicated the negotiations was the economic system of China. China was not a typical market economy at all by any measure. Significant portions of the Chinese economy were not exposed to the market mechanism. Government controls were ubiquitous, the regulations were far from transparent, and the legal system was not trustworthy. So many economic activities were organized under State-owned Enterprises (SOEs), which were closely connected to the Communist Party.

From China's point of view, accession to the global trading system was like jumping into turbulent sea. From the US point of view, allowing China into the global trading system was to accept the largest existing Communist country into the global trading system. China's seat at the WTO meant that

---

10 Any member of an international organization has a sovereign right to withdraw. Consequences may be complex and complicated, however.

the US, the architect and champion of the liberal economic order, would accommodate the strongly state-controlled Chinese-style economy. American confidence and Chinese pragmatism, and strategic calculation from both sides led to China at the WTO.

The world has kept changing its landscape since 1986, when China decided to apply for membership at the GATT. The Cold War ended with the collapse of the Soviet Union. The entire Communist bloc in Europe has ceased to exist. The command economic system of the Lenin-Stalin era lost the contest against the capitalist market economy. By 1993, the Uruguay Round produced the most ambitious multilateral trade agreement. In addition to the GATT, a new trade agreement on services, General Agreement on Trade in Services (GATS), and a new rule on dispute settlement were agreed. And the GATT was replaced by the WTO. The US negotiating strategy became more aggressive with its victory of the Cold War. Because of these ground-shaking changes, China had increasing insecurity as one of the few remaining Communist regimes, and as a growing market with pressure from other nations to open up.

Figure 1. Trade performance of Northeast Asia (unit: billion US $)

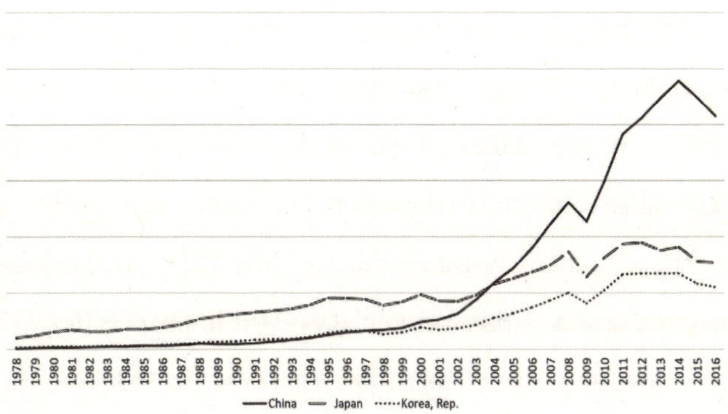

The graph shows the dramatic upsurge of the Chinese trade.

The pace of trade growth of China has been more rapid since China's entry into the WTO in 2001. The slope of curve for the Chinese after 2001 is steeper than that before 2001. China's accession to the WTO has been an inflection point.

**Source: World Bank

2. Case of iPhone in China without the WTO?

Apple's iPhone is assembled in China and shipped to the US for final consumption. The US customs can levy tariffs on iPhone imported from China. As a member of the WTO, China is granted Most Favored Nation (MFN) treatment from the US. The US cannot charge higher tariff on the imported products from China than tariff on the same products from other members of the WTO. Such an act would constitute a blatant violation of the MFN. The US and other WTO members agreed on zero tariffs for many information and technology-related products, including smart phones.

Hence, iPhone assembled in China will get zero tariff from the US.

As a thought experiment, suppose China is not a member of the WTO. What would happen to iPhone? In such a case, will the Apple continue to assemble iPhones in China? You may say "Well, it depends." Any smart CEO would want to compare the cost and benefit. In this case, the cost of assembly in China will be compared to the benefit of assembly in a country other than China. Since China is not a member of the WTO in this hypothetical example, the cost depends substantially on the import tariffs of the US on smartphones. Any person familiar with elementary calculus can easily figure out the break-even point of tariff level where the cost equals the benefit. Clearly, the higher the import tariff, the higher the cost of maintaining assembly in China. For a sufficiently high level of tariff, the CEO of Apple may decide to relocate the final assembly of iPhone to a different country. This other country would be, of course, a country with WTO membership. It may be Vietnam, which joined the WTO after a long trial. Or it may be another developing country with WTO membership, where the abundance of cheap, low-skilled labor is assured.

This counterfactual thought experiment drives home the significance of China's WTO membership. The point is not just the benefit of MFN, but also the predictability. If China is outside of the WTO system, its trading environment is assured to be full of uncertainty and risk. China's trading partner, and the US in this thought experiment, may charge pretty high tariffs on Chinese products. Those tariffs may triple to the prohibitive level over the years. (Of course, China may retaliate by erecting tariffs and other import barriers for those countries.) This sort of uncertainty is a business risk any right-minded CEO wants to make sure to avoid as much as possible. Any cost-sensitive CEO would be reluctant to assign the task of main assembly to China if China is not a member of the WTO. No WTO membership means the very visible possibility of discrimination and unpredictability. By joining the WTO, China eliminated those two negative factors for its smooth navigation of the trade waters.

The hypothetical case of iPhone assembled in China without the WTO amply illustrates the critical importance of the demand side of the equation. No matter how China may be productive in assembling products, unfavorable and unpredictable market access to the biggest consumer market in the world would not make Factory China profitable in the short run, nor sustainable in the long run.

3. Factory China: Global Value Chain in Northeast Asia

China's accession to the WTO has provided a significant institutional assurance to the Chinese economy. With its place in the WTO, China secured two wings to fly high: one old wing of economic strength, another new wing of political support. Thanks to the two solid wings, China soared higher and higher. Its ascent to the global economic landscape in the beginning of the 21st century is labelled as "Factory China." (Figure 2)

Factory China means the production network based on foreign capital from Korea, Japan, and the West, plus the supply of key parts and components from Korea and Japan, with final assembly in China.[11] Capitals (solid lines in Figure 2) are brought from neighbors (Korea and Japan) and the West (the US, the EU) in the form of foreign direct investment. To operate the final assembly in China, key parts and components (broken lines in Figure 2) are imported from Korea, and Japan. Thus assembled products are exported to the West.

Supply side of Factory China alone will not ensure its success. Producing at low cost is only necessary, not sufficient, condition for commercial success. Demand side is crucial. To have Factory China up and running, market access to the two biggest economies in the world, the US and the European Union (EU), has been critical. China's accession to the WTO solved the demand side of the Factory China equation. iPhone assembled in Shenzhen is a microcosm of Factory China.

11 The extension of "Factory China" to the broad context of Asia is "Factory Asia." The term of " Factory Asia" has been extensively used in academic literature and public discussion to capture the notion of Global Value Chain in Asia, as the title of the book and collection of papers in Choi and Lee (2014) attest.

Figure 2. Factory China

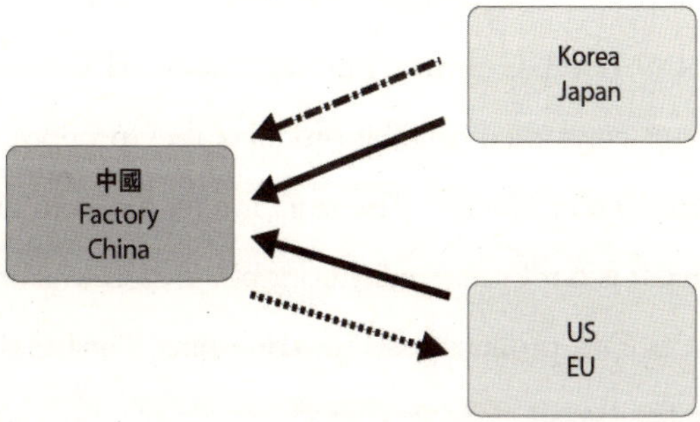

**Source: Author's illustration

Factory China is so interwoven with the West

Along with NAFTA (North American Free Trade Area) and the EU, Factory China has emerged as an important GVC in the world. Calling these economic zones as GVC, some assert, is a misnomer; they are more regional, not global, value chains. In terms of organizing production networks, NAFTA, the EU, and Factory China procure substantial portion of their parts and components from their neighbors. For instance, Mexico has emerged as the final assembly line of automobile in NAFTA, based on the supply of essential parts and components from the US and Canada. In the EU, Poland has emerged as the final assembly line of many manufacturing products, based on the supply of parts and components from Germany. Factory China relies heavily on the supply of parts and components from Korea and Japan. However, there are important differences among NAFTA, the EU, and Factory China. NAFTA and the EU also provide the biggest consumption market for the products produced by them. The US is the largest consumption market for the automobiles produced by the regional value chain of NAFTA. Germany, France, and other EU members are the most important consumers for the products they produce through the regional value chain of the EU. The story is a bit different in the case of Factory China. It is not China's neighbors, but the US which provides the biggest market for the products assembled in China. The EU is also another large market for Factory China. China's export of consumption goods reveals such a pattern. For instance, in year 2009, China exported $123 billion of consumption goods to the US, and $124.8 billion of consumption goods to the 28 members of the EU, compared to the export of $52 billion of consumption goods to Japan. In year 2015, China exported $165.7 billion of consumption goods to the US, and $140.1 billion of consumption goods to the 28 members of the EU, compared to the export of $53 billion of consumption goods to Japan.

As demonstrated in the hypothetical case of iPhone assembled in China without the WTO, the demand side matters for the success of GVC. Unfavorable and unpredictable market access to major consumer markets in the world would not make Factory China profitable in the short run, nor sustainable in the long run, no matter how China may be productive. In this perspective, China in the WTO means the Western acceptance of China in its global liberal economic order. Without securing a stable access to the US and the EU, Factory China would not have gone far enough to elevate China as the World Factory.

Figure 3. Trade in Northeast Asia: Decomposition (in billions of USD)

▲ Consumption goods ■ Intermediate goods ● Capital goods

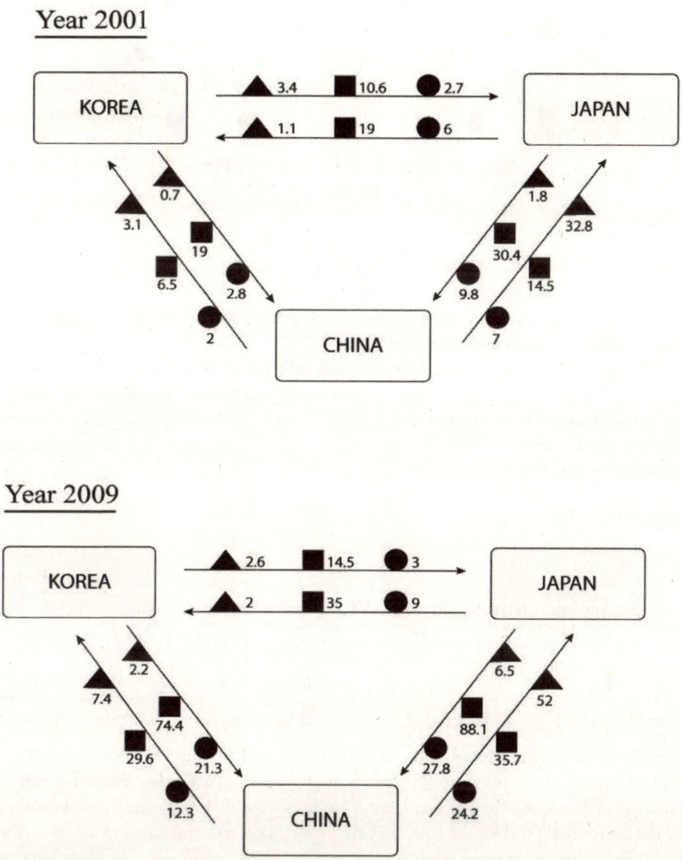

Year 2015

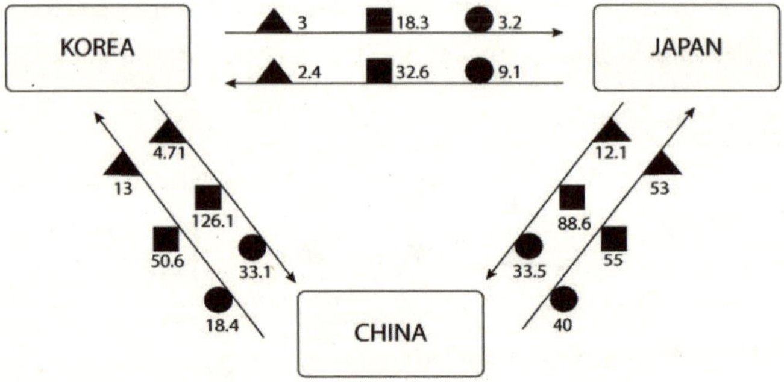

Decomposition of trade among Korea, Japan and China shows the main feature of Factory China, GVC in Northeast Asia.

China relies on the import of intermediate goods and capital goods from Korea and Japan.

Over the years, such a reliance has been increased.

Import of intermediate goods was much more significant than capital goods, with ratio of 3 to 1 (combined import of intermediate goods from Korea and Japan vs combined import of capital goods from Korea and Japan).

In particular, China's import of Korean intermediate goods has seen more increase than that of Japanese intermediate goods.

**Source: RIETI-TID

Table 2. Supply and Demand side of GVC: Comparison

	Europe	North America	Northeast Asia
Supply-side	In the region	In the region	In the region
Demand-side	In the region	In the region	Outside of the region

GVC established in Europe and North America are, in fact, Regional Value Chain because most of supply of key parts and components are supplied from the region, and major market for final products are in the region. On the other hand, GVC in Northeast Asia is more global, because major market for final products are outside of the region, while most of supply of key parts and components are from the region.

**Source: Author's own

4. Evolution of Factory China in Comparative Perspective

When China decided to come out from the "Bamboo Curtain" in the late 1970s, it did not open up all its regions for trade. Only a few regions close to the coast were opened. From the outset, the model the Chinese leaders envisioned was "assembled in China and exported to the global market." It was strikingly similar to the Japanese model and the Korean model. An important difference

should not be missed though. During its take-off stage as a trading nation, both Japan and Korea did not allow free flow of foreign investment into their domestic market. Foreign investment was allowed only in some carefully designated economic sector and area.[12] The government officials in both Japan and Korea were skeptical of foreign controls of economic activities. China was different. China embraced foreign investment.

China did not open up all of its economic sectors for foreign direct investment (FDI). It did impose strict conditions for investments such as joint venture and technology transfer. Nonetheless, compared to Japan and Korea, China's approach to FDI was more embracing. It is mainly due to absolute shortage of commercial capital and management knowhow of organizing economic activities and operating factories. To China in the early days of opening up, FDI was not only a source of needed capital, but equally

12 Eichengreen, Perkins and Shin (2012)

importantly, a source of learning about the market economy.

Comparison of Factory China with other GVCs like the EU and NAFTA reveals something interesting and remarkable.

First, the institutional aspect. Both the EU and NAFTA are supported by regional trade agreements with a dispute settlement mechanism. Factory China does not have any region-wide trade agreement among China, Japan, and Korea. Only a bilateral trade agreement between China and Korea exists.

The process of establishing and enlarging the EU has been driven by decades of negotiations among the European countries. A set of various trade agreements in products, services, investment, and sectoral policies ranging from sectors such as agriculture, IT, Intellectual Property Rights (IPR), cyberspace, competition to environment has strengthened the EU. Perhaps the process leading to the EU as a GVC is unique and may not be easily duplicated. Perhaps not! As far as institutionalization is concerned, NAFTA as a GVC is not much different from the EU. NAFTA as a GVC required a trade agreement among the US, Canada, and Mexico. Unlike the EU, which was a decades-long incremental process, the NAFTA was a sweeping and single undertaking.

Strikingly, Factory China does not enjoy such a strong institutional backup. There are a well-identifiable group of thinkers in international relations who argue that economic integration should be cemented by institutional arrangements. Without a strong institution, trade conflicts and investment disputes would not be effectively resolved. As a consequence, business people would be less willing to create a value chain encompassing the whole region. From this point of view, Factory China proves to be an exception. There is no trilateral trade agreement among China, Japan, and Korea. As a matter of fact, it was not institution which led to the establishment and strengthening of Factory China.

Factory China began without much institutional back-up. When China opened up in the late 1970s, China was not a member of the GATT, the global trading system of the day.

During the 1980s and the early 21st century when China secured a seat at the WTO, China had no guarantee of receiving no discrimination treatment in the US, the biggest market in the world. Year after year, China needed to pass the hurdle of 'normal trading relations' (NTR), which was to be unilaterally decided by US domestic politics. After the 1989 Tiananmen pro-democracy protest, allowing NTR status to China had been a hot potato topic. Non-economic considerations championed by the human right situation in China dominated the US debate of granting NTR to China.

China did not hide its uncomfortable sentiment and accused the US of "interfering with domestic, hence sovereign, issues." Despite this apparently unbearable public humiliation, Chinese leaders kept their patience and did not cross the bridge of no return in the China-US relations. What they held on to was the wisdom of "bide time and hide brightness", a strategy and wisdom offered by Deng, the architect of China's grand opening up. Were it not for this strategy, Factory China may not have grown to its ultimate place in the global economy.

It is equally important to recognize the critical mass of entrepreneurs.

Businessmen from the US dared to invest in China, despite the political uncertainty and economic unpredictability. Opening up of China meant to them the availability of the vast pool of workers at a low wage. Compared to the wage paid to American workers at home, the Chinese equivalent was worthwhile to bear the risk and take a deep plunge. They are the ones who stood with the Chinese side in the annual political ritual of the NTR debate in Washington. Entrepreneurs from Korea and Japan should not be missed either. Without their bold decision to do business in China - ideologically totally different wonderland with unforeseen economic uncertainty under the powerful Communist Party - Factory China would have been still at the drawing board of Chinese leaders. Political commitment and trade-nexus gave birth to Factory China model in the drawing board.

Second, the geopolitical risks. NAFTA and the EU are agreements among players with common values - electoral democracy and market economy. Factory China is markedly different. In terms of political system, China (the final assembly line) does not have anything common with Korea or Japan (main sources of capital, key parts, and components) nor the US (the ultimate destination of Chinese assembled products). China is a Socialist country with the Communist party dictatorship. It has been trying to adopt some elements of market economy in some segments.[13] The rule of the game is electoral democracy and market economy in Korea, Japan, and the

---

13 China has called itself 'Socialism with Chinese Characteristics'. The outside world labels China as 'State Capitalism' in contrast to 'Market Capitalism'.

US. GVCs in Europe and North America have small geopolitical risks, because countries in those regions have market economy and electoral democracy as their political system. On the other hand, GVC in Northeast Asia has inherent geopolitical risk, because China maintains a single party-based communist system, while Korea and Japan have plural party-based electoral democracy and market economy. Whenever China feels its core security interests challenged by its neighbors, China shows the tendency of extreme and hostile responses. China's trade sanction in relation to Korea's deployment of the THAAD is the case in point. Resolving non-economic disputes among China and its neighbors proved tough and is likely to be more difficult in the coming years.

GVCs in North America and Europe have been driven and shaped by trade among friends. GVC in Northeast Asia has been driven by trade among enemies. What brought enemies in the same boat is the grand strategy of "trade-security nexus" and the sense of pragmatism.[14] Between the US and China, the grand strategy of trade-security nexus played a main role. Between Korea, Japan on one side and China on the other side, the sense of pragmatism drove them into strange bedfellows.

In summary, GVC in Northeast Asia is based rather weak institutional foundation and is exposed to inherent geopolitical risks, in comparison to GVC in Europe and North America (Table 3). GVC in Europe is founded

---

14 For the role of pragmatism in shaping liberal international order in Northeast Asia, refer to Hahm (2017).

on a series of decades-long trade agreements, in addition to the WTO. GVC in North America is founded on the NAFTA, in addition to the WTO. GVC in Northeast Asia is solely founded on the WTO alone.

Table 3. Comparison of GVC

	Europe	North America	Northeast Asia
Institution	Strong	Strong	Weak
Geopolitical Risk	Small	Small	Inherent

**Source: Author's own

Trade-Security Nexus

The US decision to embrace China was at first a strategic and security-driven decision. In the early 1970s when President Nixon flew to Beijing in order to meet Mao, the supreme leader of China, what the US had in mind was to contain the Soviet Union. As long as the People's Republic of China was not willing to open and trade with the West, the US-China relations were all about security issues. The nature of relations turned into something totally different when China decided to change its statecraft by introducing some elements of market economy in the single party system.

Deep in the Cold War with the military threat of the Soviet Union, policy makers in Washington came to conclude that Beijing should be more integrated to the global economy. If China could develop its economy through engagement with the global economy, they thought, China would align its core interests more and more with the US. Hence, the door was wide open to welcome China into the liberal order. In fact, far-reaching calculation on the part of Washington power elites was that economically prosperous China would be followed by a more liberal, even perhaps democratic, China.

Immediately after its opening up to foreign investment in 1979, China joined the Bretton Woods system in the early 1980s. China's seat at the IMF and the World Bank was easily secured. However, when it came to trade relations, this was not the case. China took 15 years to earn its seat at the WTO. To a large extent, it is related to the nature of accession to these institutions. Unlike the IMF and the World Bank, which do not require substantial changes in the domestic system as conditions for entry, the WTO requires tariffs and non-tariffs negotiations. Through the negotiations for the accession to the WTO, China was required to adopt a trading system in line with the global standard, such as product classification system, custom procedure, and trade policy system. Putting in place trade remedy system of anti-dumping, countervailing duty, and safeguards was to learn and adopt the global institution. Getting familiar with the WTO dispute settlement was another important step in learning and assimilation. During those 15 year of negotiations, China has acquired and accumulated its knowledge of the global trading system. China's trading system has been reformed and upgraded along with its commitment to the WTO.

Another dimension of China's accession to the WTO deserves a closer look. By the early 1990s, the US had won the Cold War. The Communist camp of the Cold War disappeared. The Soviet Union dissolved without firing any missiles. The arch enemy of the US had collapsed. China was the largest surviving Communist state. The US could turn its side against China. It did not, however. The US continued to negotiate with China, which eventually led to China's place in the WTO.

Accepting China into the US meant that the US should accord MFN to China. Among others, it meant the US could not, in the future, leverage its trading relations to deal with China's thorny issues like human rights. In the parlance of the US trade policy, accepting China into the WTO meant Permanent Normal Trade Relations (PNTR) with China. Such a policy was supported by the Clinton (Democratic Party) and Bush (Republican Party) administrations on both foreign policy and trade policy grounds. The US policymakers were under a firm belief that extending PNTR to China and bringing Beijing into the WTO were in US national interest. These steps, they imagined, would eliminate many barriers to U.S. exports and investments in China, integrate China more deeply into the world economy, foster positive change within China, and enhance the prospects for peace and security in Asia and the world.

In the mindset of Washington, trade-security nexus was a positive-sum game. Trade Promotion Authority (TPA) of 2002 confirms this nexus.

> *The expansion of international trade is vital to the national security of the United States. Trade is critical to the economic growth and strength of the United States and to its leadership in the world. Stable trading relationships promote security and prosperity. Trade Agreements today serve the same purposes that security pacts played during the Cold War, binding nations together through a series of mutual rights and obligations. Leadership by the United States in*

international trade fosters open markets, democracy, and peace throughout the world.[15]

5. Ideology-Institution-Technology Nexus

In the actual discourse and in the analysis of international affairs, institution has been a central element. Institution is usually defined as rule of game, venue for enforcing the rule and adjudicating disputes, and forum for negotiations. A particular form of 'Institution' is so densely associated with the prevailing 'Ideology' of the leading powers. Linkage between Ideology and Institution is well established in the literature, as attested by Gilpin (1987) and Bhagwati (1988). As history shows, Ideology of the US, the emerging leading power after the World War II, was the key driving force behind the emergence of the Bretton Woods Institution (World Bank, IMF, GATT).

The role played by 'Technology' has not been fully appreciated in the existing literature of international relations in explaining the evolution of Institution. If Institution is not conducive to changing environments caused by Technology, its efficacy may be eroded, posing a severe threat to legitimacy of the Institution. Institution may facilitate or obstruct the evolution of Technology. Hence, linkage between Technology and Institution emerges. Technology also interacts with Ideology. This perspective gives rise to

15 Section 2101, Bipartisan Trade Promotion Authority Act of 2002.

Ideology-Institution-Technology Nexus (Figure 4), which is more extended than Ideology-Institution Nexus in the existing literature.

In Ideology-Institution-Technology Nexus, Institution is dependent variable, while Ideology and Technology are independent variable: Institution is the result of Ideology and Technology. Two hypotheses are derived from Ideology-Institution-Technology Nexus:

(A) A particular Institution is the outcome of a particular Ideology and a particular Technology;

(B) When Ideology changes or Technology changes, Institution is likely to face the crisis of survival.

It is important to note that Institution is not perfect. Institution may be founded under rather shaky and fragile ground. Even though it is established by the strong political will of the leading power, it may not be sustainable if it is not be strengthened. Enlargement of the membership and continual upgrading of rules are imperative for this reason.

Figure 4. Ideology-Institution-Technology Nexus

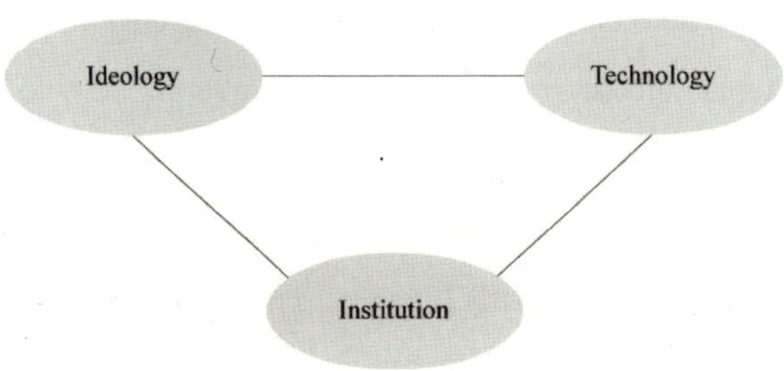

**Source: Author's illustration

6. Ideology-Institution-Technology Nexus in Northeast Asia

Apple's iPhone is a microcosm of Factory China. iPhone is invented in California, US. Its final assembly is done in Shenzhen, China. Display screen, semiconductors, memory, audio, screen controller, battery, and all other parts and components are supplied from all over the world. For each version of iPhone, Apple configures the global supply networks of those parts and components, reflecting industry dynamics and bargaining power of Apple and those suppliers. For the successful production and sale of iPhone, the two sides of equations should be solved: supply-side and demand-side. As counterfactual case of iPhone assembled in China without the WTO illustrates, the reason why the CEO of Apple could spend most of his scarce attention to figure out its suppliers-network is mainly because the demand-side of the equation has already been taken care of. China's seat at the WTO resolved the demand side problem, by securing MFN access to the global market.

Technological breakthrough played a great role in shaping Factory China. The information and communication technology (ICT) revolution of the 1990s enabled the global location of various segment of production process. Thanks to the remarkable reduction of communication cost thorough the ICT, Apple could design such an expansive global map of supplier network with final assembly in China. Without such death of distance for moving ideas, most key parts and components would have to be located nearby the final assembly line. In this regard, those enabling technology of ICT may be named as "integrating technology."

As the case of iPhone illustrates, GVC in Northeast Asia, embodied in the form of Factory China, has been driven by mutually reinforcing three factors: trade-security nexus in the belief that "trade promotes peace" (ideology), rule-based multilateral institution (institution), and ICT (technology) (Figure 5). Mutually reinforcing linkage among ideology-institution-technology nexus gave rise to thriving GVC in Europe and North America as well. Compared to GVC in Europe and North America, GVC in Northeast Asia is based on rather weak foundation of Institution. (Table 4).

GVC in Northeast Asia Since has been more firmly established since China's entry to the WTO (2001) and consolidated through increasing trade among countries in the region. Ideology-Institution-Technology Nexus in Northeast Asia is founded on rather fragile linkage. Ideology-Institution linkage bears inherent geopolitical risk, due to differences in political systems of Northeast Asia countries (Table 2). Institutional foundation is less solid, because WTO is the only institution where Korea, Japan, and China have common membership, unlike more solid institutional arrangements as in Europe or North American(Table 2). Hence, challenge was to strengthen institutional foundation.

Figure 5. Ideology-Institution-Technology Nexus in Northeast Asia (2001-2016)

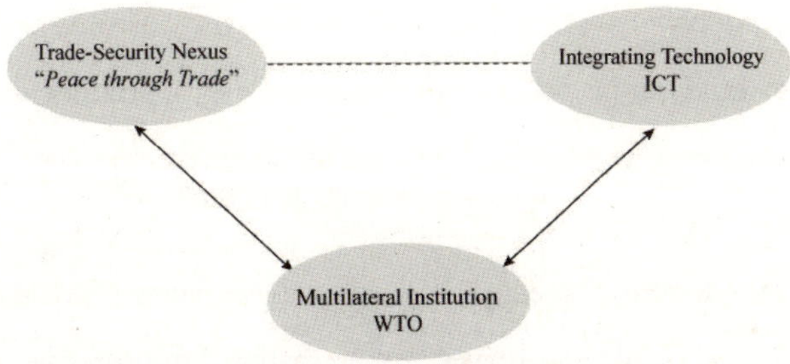

**Source: Author's illustration

Table 4. Ideology-Institution-Technology Nexus in Northeast Asia vs Europe and North America

	Europe	North America	Northeast Asia
Ideology	Trade-Security Nexus		
Technology	Integrating Technology		
Institution	WTO + Regional	WTO + Regional	WTO only, no Regional

**Source: Author's illustration

Interface between Ideology and Institution

The US acceptance of China in its liberal economic order led to the entry of China into the WTO. The multilateral trading regime, represented by the GATT (until 1994) and the WTO (after 1995), has been a cornerstone of institution. Core disciplines of the GATT/WTO are non-discrimination, fair trade, progressive liberalization, and dispute resolution. Once a nation sets its border measures (tariffs and others including technical and inspection standards), these measures would be applied to all the members without discrimination (meaning "no other will be given favors or disadvantages, and all will be treated on equal basis") - known as "most favored nation" (MFN) discipline. And once a foreign product cleared the customs and got imported, it would not be discriminated against the local product in terms of taxation or other regulations – known as "national treatment" (NT) discipline.

How are these measures set up? To begin with, each nation would set up its own measures. Eventually, however, these national measures would be negotiated. Each nation's tariffs gets lowered, and other border measures become more reasonable and less burdensome for traders. The GATT/WTO provides the venue for such negotiations. A series of multilateral trade negotiations (MTN) have been launched under the aegis of the GATT. In fact, a total of eight MTNs were conducted. The Uruguay Round (1986-1993) was the largest and the latest MTN. National border measures have gone through steady liberalization.

Through MTNs, countries would commit to certain measures. For instance, country X agrees to eliminate all existing tariffs on non-farming sectors within 5 years of the implementation of the MTN agreement. Country Y agrees to reduce all tariffs in agriculture immediately by 20 percent except for a few sensitive products (whose list should be well-defined and exhaustive). Country Z agrees to reduce the variances of commitment reflect each country's negotiating power, the level of economic development, economic structure, economic strategy, vested interests, and so on. The modus operandi of the multilateral trading system is that once a country is committed to certain measures, the measures should be applied to all the members in a non-discriminatory manner (MFN and NT). If the country does not honor its commitment (for instance, lack of implementation, reneging or backtracking), it would be subject to the disciplines of dispute settlement. The GATT/WTO agreement, the notion of a series of MTN for progressive liberalization, and the dispute settlement mechanism of the GATT/WTO are the integral part of the institution.

The multilateral institution of the GATT/WTO is a rule-based system. As long as a nation plays within the rule, the outcome of the competition among nations would be accepted. How much export a nation makes was not a concern for dispute, as long as the rule was heeded. In this sense, the GATT/WTO ensured free and open trade.[16] Take a sport contest as an analogy. In the World Cup of national competition, the outcome is determined by the competitiveness of a national team, not by non-sports factors like the political clout of a nation, economic power, cultural heritage, or rich history. In the qualifying match, Brazil may beat Germany. In the final match, Germany may upset Brazil. Only the competitiveness in playing the soccer matters. No one in the sidelines can change the outcome of the match. Perhaps grievance and dismay may motivate the Brazilian soccer team in the next World Cup to final victory. In the Master Champion of professional golf, who gets to the green jacket after the four rounds in the field of that Augusta National golf course is determined by confidence and competence,

16 "Free trade" here does not mean "zero" trade barriers at all. It means trade based on rule and without discrimination.

skill, gut, strategy, and the luck of players, not by something else. Every golfer is expected to play by the golf rule. If a rule is not honored, penalty would be imposed on the player who broke the rule.

Shallow Integration vs Deep Integration

Early observers of the globalization distinguished between "shallow" integration and "deep" integration. Shallow integration means increased trade through reduction of border measures (mainly tariffs). Deep integration means increased trade through reduction of behind-the-border measures (such as regulatory barriers). Unlike Europe or North America, Northeast Asia has yet to enter the stage of "deep" integration (Table 5).

Table 5. Shallow Integration vs Deep Integration

	EU	North America	Northeast Asia
Shallow Integration	GATT/WTO	GATT/WTO	WTO
Deep Integration	EU	NAFTA	Not there yet

**Source: Author's own

Shallow integration has been accomplished through the multilateral trade agreement of the GATT and the WTO. Since the 1990s, the world has witnessed the sudden surge of FTAs, which aimed to accord preferential market access and rules to the negotiating partners. The idea behind FTA was to seek more advantageous business opportunities beyond the WTO. Negotiating principle of single-undertaking (nothing will be agreed until everything is agreed), along with the complexities of negotiations involving economies at different stages of economic development made virtually impossible the speedy completion of trade negotiations on new issues.

The US and the EU were the two main protagonists in this FTA race. They pursued high-levels of trade liberalization beyond the WTO disciplines. They aimed for comprehensive coverage of negotiating agenda and substantial reduction of trade barriers. In principle, tariffs would be removed; the timeline for elimination for each tariff was the focal point. Liberalization commitment in various service sectors, protection of foreign investment and investor-state dispute settlement (ISDS), protection of IPR, pro-competition policy, and rules on digital commerce (often called E-Commerce) were the main features of FTAs pursued by the US and the EU.

〈Table 6〉 shows what needs to be addressed, if Northeast Asia wants to achieve deep integration. In issues like IPR, Competition, and Digital Commerce, which deem critical for enhancing the performance of national economy in the era of digital transformation, Northeast Asia simply lacks behind, in comparison to Europe and North America. In the area of conventional agenda for economic integration such as goods, services, and investment, Northeast Asia has rather weak institutional arrangement in comparison to Europe and North America, as discussed before. While Europe and North America have their region-wide FTA, which further improves and consolidates trading architecture among them, Northeast Asia has yet to have its equivalent to Europe and North America.

Table 6. Agenda for Deep Integration

	Europe	North America	Northeast Asia
Goods	WTO + FTA	WTO + FTA	WTO only
Services	WTO + FTA	WTO + FTA	WTO only
Investment	Strong	Strong	Weak
IPR	Yes	Yes	No
Competition	Yes	Yes	No
Digital Commerce	Yes	Yes	No

**Source: Author's own

7. Institution-Ideology-Technology Nexus in Northeast Asia under Challenges

The Institution-Ideology-Technology Nexus, which has taken deep root in GVC in Northeast Asia, is not as solid as it can be. Compared with other GVCs in Europe or North America, Factory China has been built on weak institution. Despite less solid institutional foundation and inherent geopolitical risk, Factory China has gradually and steadily emerged and became a major modus operandi of GVC in Northeast Asia. What has been lacking in Northeast Asia was overcome by the grand strategy of "trade-security" nexus and pragmatism.

In retrospect, the period of 1978 to 2008 was the time of China's peaceful rise through the expansion of Factory China. Even though China decided to open to the world in 1978, there was no meaningful institutional foundation for trade and investment in China for a considerable time. From 1978 to 2001, China was outside of the global trading system. In theory, China could withdraw from international trade by reneging its market opening promise and unilaterally upending liberalization measures. In case of such eventuality, Korea, Japan, and the US would have little to recourse except political pressure.[17]

After 2001, since China's accession to the WTO, the WTO has been the main institution among trading partners. There were no other bilateral trade agreements between China and the three countries - Korea, Japan and the US - and there were no regional trade agreements among those countries. Korea and China agreed to the bilateral FTA only much later, in 2014. Trilateral FTA negotiations among China, Japan, and Korea were launched in March 2013. Several rounds of negotiations until this day have not led to any substantial progress toward the completion due to asymmetric position in market opening and rule making.

In the area of investment, both Japan and Korea negotiated a basic bilateral investment treaty (BIT) with China more than 20 years ago: the BIT between Japan and China was reached in 1988, and the BIT between Korea and China in 1992. The China-Japan-Korea (CJK) investment agreement tried to align the investment standards of the three countries more closely, including provisions on performance requirements, transparency, and IPR. These advancements are particularly important for Japan; the 1988

---

17 Garlic dispute between Korea and China, which took place in 2000, is a case in point. The dispute would have been settled more amicably, if China was a member of the WTO. For details, refer to Choi (2005).

Japan-China BIT lacked such provisions, while the 1992 Korea-China BIT was amended in 2007 to include new obligations in these areas.

Factory China without Deep Institution

According to Richard Baldwin, "deep" disciplines are necessary to have an effective GVC.[18]

> *"One can think of a Toyota Land Cruiser not as a vehicle but rather as a bundle of Japanese labor, capital, innovation, and managerial, marketing, engineering, and production know-how. In 1982, the Land Cruiser could be exported to any nation without regard to the destination's property rights because it was basically impossible to unbundle the inputs. Toyota's intangible property rights were protected by la in Japan and physics abroad. Now things are quite different.*
>
> *Today, Toyota assembles Land Cruisers in several nations and sources the parts and components from factories around the world, including many developing nations. Since the parts all have to fit together seamlessly, Toyota does not rely only on local know-how. It combines Japanese capital, Japanese innovation, and Japanese know-how with local labor when producing parts for its international supply chain. The result is that physics provides much less protection for Toyota's intangible property.*
>
> *Production unbundling creates new vulnerabilities to intangible property. Deep disciplines are necessary to ensure Toyota's property rights are respected in the developing nations that get the Toyota factories."*

18 Quoted from Baldwin (2016) p. 238

These disciplines are "institutions" in the framework of this book. Bringing high-quality, competitively prices goods to customers in a timely manner is a defining element of global competitiveness. The successful execution of this task requires international coordination of production facilities via the continuous two-way flow of goods, people, ideas, and investment. For instance, connecting factories often involves time-sensitive shipping, world-class telecoms, and short-term movement of managers and technicians; tariffs and other border measures matter for every shipping to different nations for the next task. Hence, to strengthen the GVC, it becomes critical to make it easier to do business abroad, and to ensure that international production facilities remain connected. Under this line of reasoning, the 21st century trade policies have the following list of prioritie s[19]: Competition policy, Movement of capital, IPR, Investment measures, and Business mobility (assured short-term visas for managers and technicians)

Factory China has evolved without much of deep disciplines. In a positive way, Factory China has evolved to the current peak despite lack of deep disciplines. This brings up a deep question. "How far can Factory China advance without deep institution?" Answering this question is what motivated this book.

---

19 Baldwin named this work as the trade-investment-services-intellectual property nexus. (Baldwin 2016, pp. 238-239)

iPhone Case Revisited

Before moving on, let us take the case of iPhone again. The supply-side of iPhone has been shaped by advances in ICT, while the demand side of iPhone was taken care of by China's membership at the WTO. As argued before, iPhone represents a microcosm of Factory China, which is in essence the nexus of US-led ideology of globalization - institution (WTO) - technology.

This ideology-institution-technology nexus is not something that was built in a short time. The nexus as such was the outcome of decades of evolution. Moreover, the nexus is subject to noise and disturbance. If the nexus is strong, it would be resilient and survive. Otherwise, it may be damaged and broken into pieces. To drive this point home, let's try another thought experiment.

What if the US decides not to import iPhone from China due to growing concern on labor rights? You may imagine mounting pressures from NGOs on their investigation of working condition in the assembly lines in China. Beijing becomes upset, stating that labor rights issue is a domestic issue for China to handle, not a concern for the US. Furious China brings the complaint to the WTO. Can the WTO handle this issue?

Short answer is "No." The WTO has no jurisdiction in this matter. Issues like this fall on the agenda of so-called "Labor and Trade," which lies outside of the WTO disciplines. Leeway may be explored through "Exception." Again, adjudication of the complaint will be complicated. If China wins the case, the US would not implement. Even if China loses the case, it is inconceivable that China would just accept the decision and take trade sanctions. Setting aside legal judgement, the crux of the matter is whether China will have difficulty in keeping iPhone assembly inside of China in either case of legal coin loss. Foreseeing this possibility, which is not actually unrealistic at all, what would be the choice of Beijing?

Take another hypothetical situation. What if Apple invents a new iPhone, named iPhone Z, which has an automated drone function and a 3-D printer function? And Apple continues to assemble iPhone Z in China. The US military becomes highly alert because of security concerns. They present the case to the US Congress that iPhone Z should not be assembled in China. Apple is under mounting pressure to relocate its assembly from China to the US.

The morale of this tale is the same as the previous one. In the changing external environment, Factory China will face treacherous currents and headwinds. As long as China stays on the course with Chinese-style state-dominant economic system (State Capitalism), the external forces would continue to request China to embrace more elements of the market system. Otherwise, China will confront a huge bill. Further embracing market elements would be challenging. Top leaders in Beijing will regard such choice as a humiliation or conspiracy: Humiliation to the national pride, and conspiracy to topple down the Communist regime. Surely, some reformers out there present a strong case for embracing the road for the future of China. Henceforth, the contest in Beijing has been, and will be, the battle between reform-minded globalists versus status-quo nationalists.

Factory China will hit its wall soon. When it hits the wall, its choice is stark: either jump and climb, or give up. Strategic policymakers will come up with other strategies. "Simply ignore the wall. We will become bigger and bigger. Eventually the wall becomes smaller than us." "Jump and climb" means the adoption of the game rule set by others. "Give up" means the end of reform. "Ignore the wall" is about changing the game from catch-up to a play with China's own rule.

From the perspective of Japan and Korea, who have been enjoying the low-hanging fruits from Factory China, the game also becomes complicated. Now that low-hanging fruits become increasingly scarce, doing business in China becomes more challenging. Thanks to its remarkable catch-up, China itself became confident, unruly, and assertive. Japan and Korea find two groups of different strategies: "build a higher wall" and "bridge."

"Build a higher wall" strategy intends to set barriers which are high for China. "Bridge" strategy means helping out China. Both strategies have gains and risks. Successful "build a higher wall" strategy would give rise to deep integration and strengthened institutionalization in the sphere of the liberal order. Failure of "higher wall-building" strategy means hostility and fragmentation. On the other hand, successful bridge strategy means less tension and harmonization. However, it also means the prevalence of State Capitalism and illiberal order in Northeast Asia. How will this game unfold? The rest of this book will take a closer look at the evolution of strategic contests and a glimpse into the future.

3 Setting the Stage towards Deep Integration:

The First Decade of the New Millennium

The first decade of the new millennium in Northeast Asia started with a renewed excitement. At last, China became a member of the multilateral trading system of the WTO. Korea, Japan, and China now had common rules for trade. From the view point of Korea and Japan, it meant they could resolve trade conflicts with China through the WTO. If one recalls the fiasco of the Korea-China trade dispute on garlic, China's seat at the WTO meant more measured adjudication and resolution of trade conflicts. The problem was that the institution of the WTO was already becoming less relevant to govern increasingly complex trade relations in the 21st century. Speedy transformation of the global economy into a more densely interconnected economy through digital technology implied that trade rules of the WTO, mainly confined to the analogue economy of goods and services, were incapable of addressing emerging contemporary trade issues. At the same time, ever-increasing flow of cross-border foreign investments required proper protection for investors in foreign territories, while the WTO agreement was silent on this matter.

In the era of post-Cold War global economy, a growing number of emerging states were vying to attract foreign investments. A stylized fact of the FDI attraction game was to promise favorable treatment to foreign investors. From a state's point of view, FDI attraction was a zero-sum game: If Thailand is successful in having an automobile factory from Toyota with annual capacity of 300,000 productions, the equivalent amount of investment disappears for Malaysia and Vietnam. Hence, competition among emerging countries was fierce. The list of carrots to attract FDI gets longer: special tax break, provision of free land, construction of speedy access to stations, ports, and airports, guarantee of no labor union, and so on. Such special provisions often backfired. Civil activists and the media highlight negative effects of FDI, blaming it for impairing the environment, degrading labor conditions, and driving out local companies of their home market. On the other hand, some states came up with conditions for FDI, such as mandatory technology transfer, joint venture requirement, local content requirement, and restrictions on transfer of money out of the country. This practice is known as "performance requirement" in the parlance of trade policy. Foreign investors were pressed between hostile civil activists and opportunistic host states. It was imperative that trade policy makers properly deal with the issue. With the Factory China model up and running, investors from Korea, Japan, and other countries were increasingly aware of the risks associated with their investment into China.

1. Shallow Integration

On this pressing issue, the WTO was silent. There was no investment-related agreement in the WTO. In fact, during the mid-1990s, immediately after the establishment of the WTO, attempts were made to create an agreement on investment, in the name of Multilateral Agreement on Investment (MAI) among OECD (Organization for Economic Cooperation and Development) members. The idea at the drawing board was a two-step approach: first, the creation of MAI among OECD members, and second, the extension of MAI to the WTO. MAI negotiations had seen some progress. A draft agreement was made and it looked like the deal was imminent. While the negotiations were under way, trade officials confronted opposition forces. Civil activists protested, alleging that cultural diversity, most importantly in the audio-visual sector including films, would be in jeopardy. The opposition was mainly from France and French-speaking region of Canada. Trade officials could not overcome the opposition.[20]

Because of this institutional background, investment-related arrangement among states was mainly bilateral. Investors from Japan and Korea were protected by bilateral arrangements, known as the Bilateral Investment Treaty (BIT). At the early phase of diplomatic normalization with China, BITs were agreed between Japan and China in 1988, and between

20 As it turns out, this opposition against the MAI was the first anti-globalization movement on the global scale.

Korea and China in 1992. These BITs had some important elements for investor protection, including ISDS mechanism. Under ISDS, a foreign investor can challenge the host state in international courts to settle complaints related to alleged discriminatory practices. The system of ISDS has been operating since the 1960s. The fact that China, a socialist country, accepted the idea of ISDS implied that China was eager to attract FDI as an integral part of its economic development strategy. However, those bilateral BITs lacked detailed procedures, leaving substantial parts of ISDS at the discretion of Chinese government officials, outside of the agreements. Performance requirement was also quite burdensome for foreign investors. Most importantly, the presence of bilateral BITs did not mean more open access to various sectors in China. China continued to maintain a limited number of sectors for foreign investors.

Flow of FDI in East Asia has been uni-directional, from the developed countries to the developing and emerging countries. FDI from Japan to China and FDI from Korea to China were steadily on the rise, while FDI from China to Japan and FDI from China to Korea were stagnant and remained at low level.

Further Opening of China

For the sustainability of Factory China, what was in need was not only investor protection but also investment liberalization. When China decided to undertake "opening up and reform," it did not embrace the big bang approach, unlike the Eastern European countries after the collapse of their communist regimes in the early 1990s. Steps taken by China were gradual and cautious. They opened selected coastal areas for foreign investors. Even in these selected areas, not every business activities were open for foreign investment. The Chinese Communist Party had complete control of the economy and decided areas and sectors for international investment. The list of sectors and regions was getting longer over time, but slowly. With the entry into the WTO, China secured non-discriminatory market access to the global market. Through accession negotiations, China opened up some sectors for foreign investment. Notwithstanding, China was still an economy with so many restrictions.

To the Western powers, China was regarded as taking advantage of its asymmetrical market access situation. While the Western markets were wide open for Chinese products, China kept closing its market from foreign products and, more importantly, foreign investment. Notwithstanding this perception, during the most of the first decade of the 21st century, the Western approach to China was less confrontational, and more accommodating and engaging. In the global stage, China coined the word of "the Peaceful rise of China" and heavily promoted. In return, the US demanded China to be a major stakeholder, not just a passive member of the global system. With the continuing rise of China, Washington became more explicit in its demand. The jargon of G2, which became a household name after the 2008 global financial crisis, was coined to request China to bear more responsibility in the global stage. Pressure was built on China to take a more active role in the global fight against global warming and global imbalance. The unmistakable implication was for China to open up further.

Whereas market opening pressures from the outside, in the name of reciprocity and fairness, were rather meek, voices of further opening up and reform were also clearly audible from the inside. When Premier Wen Jiabao characterized the soundness of the Chinese economy with the "four 'uns'" - unstable, unbalanced, uncoordinated, and unsustainable - his assessment carried the tone of grave concern. At the same time, a sense of complacency was also felt. The rapidly-industrializing China gave rise to a new group of vested interests. The omnipresence of powerful SOEs in the Chinese economy helped consolidate vested interests. They were afraid of competing with foreign counterparts in their sphere of business, while they wanted to go global in order to increase their influence and scale up their operation. Inside of China, contest between globalists and nationalists was taking place.[21] China found itself between reform pressures and vested interest. This conundrum was precisely the situation China confronted. Which direction will China take?

Delayed reform and opening up would be costly to China. Even though the continuing rise of China would attract investors from Korea and Japan, delayed improvement in investor protection and investment liberalization would eventually catch on. Other emerging countries in East Asia were vying to attract FDIs from Japan and Korea. They raced to promise more carrots

21 Refer to Phillusbury (2016). Wang Jisi (2011) from Peking University offers his view on this contest.

and sugars. China was competing with these countries.

2. Different Steps Towards Same Goals

Understanding the necessity of improving and upgrading investment rule, China, Japan, and Korea began to move on. Even though the new multilateral trade negotiations, officially named as the DDA, launched in December 2001, the three countries in Northeast Asia were fully aware of the limitation of the DDA: the DDA would not deliver a global rule on investment issues. Hence, they decided to create a trilateral investment agreement amongst them (CJK Investment Treaty). Moreover, they wanted to establish an FTA amongst them (CJK FTA). Those were goals set in the long-term horizon. In the case of successful conclusion of both the CJK Investment Treaty and the CJK FTA, Northeast Asia would have a rather solid institutional set up, something closer to the NAFTA and the EU. Steps taken by Korea, Japan, and China towards these visions proved extremely cautious. So far, so many expected stops, unexpected pauses, and procrastination occurred, and there is still a long way to go.

In the case of the CJK Investment Treaty, the three countries spent most of the first decade of the 21st century on feasibility analysis conducted by scholars and experts without involving government officials. More than six years of the private sector-led feasibility study was followed by the next stage of another feasibility study with the engagement of government officials. When the second stage was completed, the second decade of the new millennium began. In the early 2010s, China, Japan and Korea accomplished to complete negotiations and signed on a trilateral investment agreement. Compared to bilateral investment agreements among them, the trilateral treaty showed modest improvement, reflecting a compromise between defensive China and aggressive Japan and Korea.

While undertaking these negotiating initiatives, Korea, Japan, and China showed their political commitment in promoting institutionalization of trilateral cooperation by establishing the Trilateral Cooperation Secretariat (TCS) in 2011. TCS was set up in Seoul, Korea. TCS runs on a rather small budget and staff. It does not undertake any analysis on the trilateral trade issues, nor sponsor the CJK FTA negotiations. Its main function is to promote and outreach the significance of trilateral cooperation.

3. Game for Strategic Preemption

China, Japan, and Korea did not swiftly move to negotiate the CJK FTA. During the first decade of the 21st century, the three countries spent their political assets and negotiating resources in developing their own FTA network. Interestingly, such FTA network building competition among the three countries was more reactionary than proactive.

The first FTA undertaken by any of the three countries was only negotiated late in the 20th century - Korea's FTA negotiation with Chile in 1999. The Korea-Chile FTA talks were concluded in 2002, and the agreement went into force only in 2004. Japan's first FTA was with Singapore, which became effective in 2002. China became interested in FTA only after becoming a member of the WTO. Around these times, bilateral FTAs became fashionable and popular as a policy tool to increase market access. The academic circle debated the desirability of FTAs. The debate boiled down to "spaghetti bowl effect" vs "competitive liberalization." Some contended that FTA was not free trade but preferential trade, putting non-negotiating countries at a disadvantage, thereby impairing the very sprit of multilateralism. On the other hand, some argued that FTA would provoke competition among countries to liberalize.

East Asian countries, as major beneficiaries of the multilateral global trading system, stood outside of FTAs for some time. At the turn of the new millennium, none of Northeast Asian countries had any bilateral FTAs. Japan and Korea did not have the concept of FTA in their map of trade strategy. In their mindset, FTA meant the opening of the agriculture sector, an extremely unpopular political act, as their experience in the Uruguay Round (1986-1993) exemplify.

As major trading nations, Korea and Japan have always wanted to secure enhanced market access in foreign countries. Other countries demanded the opening of agriculture market from Korea and Japan. The agriculture sector was adamantly resisting opening up. Political cost of opening up the agriculture sector was dearly high due to domestic political institutional arrangement. Farmers were exercising more political clout than their fair share. Changing external situations brought a case for action. The 1997 Asian Financial Crisis and growing number of FTAs on the global stage became the agent of change. For Korea and Japan, just sticking to the WTO regime as the only trade liberalization mechanism was not keeping up with the times. In particular, Korea came to sober awareness that Korea should dramatically enhance its credibility in the global business community in order to bail out the Korean economy from the ongoing-financial crisis. For the first time, Korean policy makers turned to FTA as a trade strategy.

This changing strategy did not bring major shifts to the FTA in an aggressive manner, though. The momentum created by changing circumstances was not monumental enough to upset the existing domestic political economic equilibrium immediately. Resistance from vested interests was strong. Agriculture was a major source of opposition. Other import-competing sectors voiced their concern as well. The status quo was under pressure. However, a new balance was to be found. Trajectories from the status quo to a new equilibrium were to be maped out. New vision was imperative. Strategies to achieve the vision were in need. Roadblocks and obstacles were to be identified. Communications were essential to forge consensus among stakeholders. And, who would take action? Different responses to these key questions would translate into many different trajectories, and to different equilibria.

In the first decade of the new millennium, the main driving force for the FTA race in Northeast Asia was the hope of trade preemption and the fear of trade diversion. By negotiating an FTA with a foreign country, government policy makers intended to create a more favorable market access condition for their products and services vis-à-vis like products and services from competing countries. An example will be helpful to explain the mindset of policymakers. Consider the case of automobiles from Japan and Korea competing in a developing country. As a member of the WTO, this country has an MFN tariff - which is identical for all WTO members - set at 15%. So, all auto imports from Korea and Japan are levied 15% tariff for each auto. Suppose this country negotiates an FTA with Korea, and agrees to eliminate the 15% MFN tariff within 5 years from entry into force. This new situation would give rise to more favorable trade conditions for the Korean auto industry, and a disadvantageous situation for Japanese automobiles - trade preemption effect for Korean autos, while trade diversion effect for Japanese autos. From the exporting firm's perspective, having an FTA with a foreign country is equivalent to a windfall of export subsidy. Thanks to export subsidy in the form of the FTA, the price of the firm's product in the foreign market becomes cheap.

Trade preemption and trade diversion are two sides of the same coin. Trade preemption may not last forever, or even not that long. Its duration depends on the trade strategy of competing countries. In the example above, trade preemption effect which Korea intends to create may be short lived if Japan negotiates an FTA with this foreign country in due course. Then, the trade diversion effect for Japanese autos would not be that long. What has happened in the policy space of Northeast Asia trade strategy was pretty much along the mix of trade preemption and trade diversion. Trade diversion effects from the NAFTA in 1994 and the Mexico - EU FTA in 2000 were of deep concern for the Japanese automobile and electronics industries. Japan tried to counter the preferential treatment of their American and European competitors in one of Japan's most important export market. The outcome was the Japan-Mexico FTA. NAFTA also prompted the Korean government to pursue FTAs with Canada, Mexico, and the United States to cope with the adverse effect of trade diversion.

Fear of Trade Diversion

The same economic rationale drove the FTA race among Korea, Japan, and China with the Association of Southeast Asian Nations (ASEAN). In October 2003, Japan and ASEAN signed a framework agreement for FTA. This move prompted China and Korea to join the race to make an FTA with ASEAN due to fear of trade diversion effect. The Japan-ASEAN FTA came into force in December 2008, whereas the China-ASEAN FTA came into force in July 2005 for trade in goods, July 2007 for trade in services, and January 2010 for investment. The Korea-ASEAN FTA came into force in June 2007 for trade in goods, May 2009 for trade in services, and September 2009 for investment.

FTA strategies of Japan and Korea had major opposition from the agriculture sector. Policy makers were keenly aware of the sensitivity. For this reason, even though Japan signed a few FTAs starting from its agreement with Singapore, the formal name was not FTA, but Economic Partnership Agreement (EPA), with substantial carve out of the agriculture sector from trade liberalization commitment. Japan had EPA with Mexico and Malaysia. Japan also launched talks with Korea in December 2003. The bilateral talks between Japan and Korea broke down after less than a year, however. The reason behind the collapse was irreconcilable differences in FTA approach. Japan did not want to liberalize its agriculture industry extensively, whereas Korea pressed for substantial liberalization of the Japanese agriculture sector. Korea wanted to negotiate an FTA with Japan. Japan thought Korea accepted the idea of EPA with Japan. From the Japanese point of view, Korea's boldness in market liberalization was incomprehensible.

Korea-Japan FTA Talks: Premature Attempt?

Despite close and interdependent economic relations, Korea and Japan did not have close institutional underpinnings other than the WTO. The 1997 Financial Crisis brought about a new momentum. Korea came to realize the importance of forging a closer tie with the financial power of Japan. Import source diversification is a case in point. Korea maintained a list of import source diversification, which de facto limited the import of Japanese electronics and consumer products. From Japan's view point, this measure was a blatant violation of the non-discrimination principle (MFN to be exact) of the multilateral trading system.

Both Korea and Japan wished to enhance their economic relations into a strong institutional binding. The vision of the Korea-Japan FTA emerged as an integral element. Joint study groups were set up to check the feasibility and sensitivity of such an arrangement.

The formal negotiations for the bilateral FTA between Korea and Japan began in 2003. In the fall of 2003, President Roh Moo-hyun from Korea and

Prime Minister Koizumi from Japan officially agreed to start FTA negotiations. FTA negotiations formally began in December 2003 and unsuccessfully ended a year later in December 2004, after just six rounds of negotiations.

A major cause for the standstill in the Korea-Japan FTA talks was disagreements over the opening of Japan's agricultural and fishery markets.[22] Despite the agreement to engage in comprehensive negotiation, both parties faced an obsta

cle. The negotiators from the two sides could not agree on the coverage of the negotiation, hence preventing the negotiation from actually starting. The Korean FTA delegates offered 95% coverage on industrial products and 90% coverage on agricultural products. The Japanese delegates were willing to offer 100% coverage on industrial products but refused to state a coverage figure for agricultural products. Ultimately, the negotiation broke down when the Korean government refused to negotiate without receiving a coverage figure for agricultural products. From the Korean government's perspective, concluding an FTA with Japan that excluded a majority of agricultural items was politically unfeasible.

---

22 Choi and Oh (2011) argues: "The failed case of Korea-Japan FTA illustrates how Japan's fragmented domestic trade governance enables farm interests to wield disproportionately large influence on Japan's overall FTA agenda. From the onset, domestic trade governance had a clear impact on the negotiating strategies of both parties."

No Japanese political leader gave a clear signal to their negotiators to broaden the agenda at the table. Vested interests of technocrats were at the driver's seat. Breakdown of the Korea-Japan FTA negotiations shows vividly the narrow zone for mutually acceptable trade agreement between Korea and Japan without deep political commitment. In the early stage of the new millennium, Japan was not yet primed for deep integration with a close neighbor. Most importantly, political leadership was in short supply.

4. Korea's Bold and Aggressive FTA Approach: Game Changer

Until half-way through the first decade of the new millennium, Korea, Japan, and China have not achieved much significant progress in their pursuit of FTAs. Despite the growing awareness of the necessity for more institutionalization on investment rule, the three countries did not have political resolve to launch trilateral talks. The three countries had a strong manufacturing sector. Japan and Korea were global powers in the heavy and chemical industries, and China was the world factory for labor intensive products. Securing access to the advanced countries was the key for their success. Despite a strong necessity of creating trade preemption and avoiding trade diversion, policy makers were not effective in overcoming domestic opposition from import-competing sector.

Both Korea and Japan heavily protected and subsidized their declining agricultural sectors. Although small in number, well-organized farmers mount a formidable opposition against agricultural liberalization. These farmers benefit from favorable public opinion and politicians who are reluctant to upset their rural electorates. Korean farmers had far more to lose from agricultural liberalization than Japanese farmers. The majority of Korean farmers are full-time farmers who derive most of their income from agricultural production. About 80% of Japanese farmers, however, are part-time farmers who predominantly rely on nonagricultural income.[23] Agricultural liberalization had a more immediate and harmful impact on the income of Korean farmers unless the government heavily supplements their incomes. Due to the lack of adequate welfare system in the rural area, the Korean government had greater constraint in pursuing agricultural liberalization than the Japanese government. Given these conditions, one would expect the Japanese government to have a more favorable attitude toward agricultural liberalization than the Korean government. What has happened was the exact opposite of this common sense conjecture. The KORUS FTA was a case in point.

In the summer of 2003, Korea's Ministry of Foreign Affairs and Trade (MOFAT) came up with an "FTA roadmap" that envisioned wiring Korea with a global network of FTAs to improve Korea's trading leverage vis-a-vis foreign countries. According to the roadmap, forging FTAs with Korea's

23.Choi and Oh (2011)

major trading partners such as the US, EU, China, and Japan were top priorities. It is important to note that among these four large trading partners, three are major exporters of agricultural products. Prior to the establishment of MOFAT in 1998, the chances of the US, EU, and China emerging as top priority FTA partners were very low. Strong resistance from Ministry Of Agriculture most likely would have prevented the Korean government from pursuing FTAs with any of these countries. Yet, by 2003, MOFAT acquired the capacity to set Korea's trade agenda based on the broader national economic interest. Concerns over agricultural liberalization no longer dictated the selection of Korea's FTA partners.

Even though the Korean government designated the US as a potential FTA partner, the prospect of a KORUS FTA seemed rather poor. First, the US was suspicious of the Korean government's ability to deliver, as was the case in previous BIT talks. Second, the Korean government would face severe domestic opposition, especially from farm interests. And third, President Roh Moo-hyun was perceived as a left-wing and anti-American politician with a hostile stance toward neoliberal trade policy.

Korea's Bold Approach to the US for FTA

Korea's initiative of launching an FTA negotiation with the US took Japan and China by surprise. Decision to negotiate an FTA with the US also took the very powerbase of the Korean government by great surprise. From the moment of announcing such a decision in early 2006, the entire Korean society became sharply divided into pros and cons. The successful conclusion of the Korea-US FTA ("KORUS") seemed an impossible idea. It was a journey against all odds.[24]

An opposition consisting of import-competing interests such as the farming sector, film industry, and anti-American civil groups waged anti-KORUS movements throughout the negotiation process. These opposition forces criticized the KORUS as a neo-liberal policy that would worsen income distribution. Angry protesters were an inescapable part of the KORUS negotiations. They stormed the venues of domestic hearings by physical force and disrupted the process of domestic deliberation. Every round of trade negotiations between the Korean government and the US government found protesters, regardless of the place, be it in the soil of Korea or of the US. A group of Korean protesters travelled all the way to Washington, DC, Seattle, and Montana to voice their opposition. Throughout the whole negotiation process, the Korean negotiators had to wage a tough two-level negotiations - negotiating with the US, and with the Korean opposition groups.

The KORUS produced substantial liberalization of the agricultural sector. Tariff concession covered 99.2% of agricultural and fishery products. The Korean government agreed to immediately grant duty-free status to two-thirds of agricultural imports from the US and gradually eliminate tariffs and import quotas on the remaining agricultural products within 10

24 For the analysis of controversies surrounding the KORUS, refer to Choi (2006).

years. From the viewpoint of the Japanese government, Korea's decision to open up its agriculture sector to gain improved access to the US was something beyond comprehension. It was mixed feelings of disbelief and astonishment. Opening up the farming sector to the US to enhance market access was something unthinkable in the policy circles of Tokyo. Mere economic calculus would not upset the status quo.

The KORUS: Against All Odds

From the Korean side, several factors contributed to success: leadership, domestic governance, and communication strategy. Completion of the KORUS required all of these factors as well as an effective interplay among these factors. Just note that the Korean government of President Roh, which decided to go ahead with the idea of having an FTA with the US, had come to power on the rising wave of anti-American sentiment. The Roh government also inherited the legacy of the previous administration, which was the failure to conclude the BIT talks with the US. The BIT, if successful, would have been a chapter of the FTA. The BIT talks between Korea and the US could not move to the finish line in the midst of stubborn opposition from the film sector. As it turned out, the film sector was an integral element of Kim Dae-jung's power base. President Roh Moo-hyun had a common power base, including the film sector. How would Washington be receptive to the idea of the KORUS when the previous administration of Korea did not manage to complete a smaller package than the FTA? What if the FTA talks collapse again? It would be a devastating blow to US-Korea relations. Risks of expected and unexpected unknowns were high.

The initiation of the KORUS meant the two-front task of confronting and meeting expected opposition from the political power base, and convincing the US to come to the bargaining table. To bring a reluctant and even suspicious US to the table, the Korean government spent the entire year of 2005 to create a fertile ground to launch the KORUS FTA. Foremost, Korea aimed to resolve pending bilateral issues between the US and Korea. The two most important issues to the US were reductions in Korean screen quota and resumption of US beef import. Also, Korea was fully aware that the US would not be interested in an FTA without substantial agricultural liberalization. All these were uphill tasks. Interplay between leadership and the executive branch in full charge of tasks played a decisive role.[25]

Although the MOFAT had all the negotiating authority, sectoral resistance was strong. Among those, the Ministry of Agriculture (MOA) stood out. In ironing out differences among Ministries, MOFAT sought out the support of President Roh Moo-hyun. MOFAT presented the economic and strategic case for the KORUS. It argued that the potential benefit from the KORUS was too big to squander, outweighing any negative effects from the comprehensive liberalization of the agricultural sector that excluded rice. It went on to argue that an FTA with the US would dramatically enhance

25 Choi and Oh (2011)

Korea's negotiating leverage with other countries.

President Roh was persuaded by the logic behind the KORUS and gave unwavering political support. Despite opposition from even his own ruling party, he agreed to cut annual screen quota from 40% to 20% as a precondition to the KORUS talks. The Korean government also lifted the ban on US beef import. Most importantly, President Roh maintained the view that the Korean agricultural sector could not avoid market opening in Korea's race to enhance global competitiveness. He firmly believed that the KORUS was a national agenda that should not be subject to myopic sectoral interests and partisan ideology.

While the strategic vision and nimble execution of MOFAT was instrumental in launching the KORUS, Korean negotiators confronted much more formidable obstacles during the negotiation process. The most difficult sector was agriculture; Korean negotiators were caught between strong US demands for complete opening and vehement domestic opposition. The Korean negotiating strategy was to offer all agricultural products on the negotiating table except for rice, and negotiate to secure safeguards and longer phase-out periods. During the entire negotiating phase of the KORUS FTA, the Ministerial Meetings for coordination effectively ironed out internal differences and worked out domestically acceptable negotiating positions for the Korean negotiators.[26]

---

26 Choi and Oh (2011) accounts for the coordination process in detail

5. Asymmetry in Approach[27]

In the first decade of the new millennium, the Korean path toward trade preemption was quite different from the Japanese path. This asymmetry is striking, considering both countries' similar economic structure in terms of weak farming sector and strong external dependency. What has caused such asymmetry?

Political constraints, foreign pressures for liberalization, and economic factors undoubtedly influence government positions on trade policies. More often than not, mutually exclusive sectoral pressures came to the fore, resulting in intense inter-ministerial conflicts. Without an institutional mechanism to coordinate inter-ministerial conflicts, it is difficult for governments to liberalize sensitive sectors. Hence, cohesive trade governance - in other words, centralized authority over trade negotiations and effective inter-ministerial coordination mechanisms - is a necessary condition that enables governments to pursue agricultural liberalization. Given the prior conditions of cohesive domestic trade governance, centralized political leadership provides the most conducive environment for a successful FTA negotiation that substantially liberalizes the agricultural sector.

27 Discussion in this section heavily draws on Choi and Oh (2011), (2017).

Korea: Cohesive Trade Governance

Throughout the first decade of the 21st century, Korea maintained a centralized trade policy-making structure. The authority to formulate and negotiate on foreign trade policies for all sectors (including agriculture) rested within the Office of the Minister for Trade (OMT) under MOFAT.

The head of OMT, the Minister for Trade, had full authority to direct trade policy-making and negotiations. The centralization of the trade policy-making and negotiation authority into the pro-trade OMT significantly weakened the voice of protectionist interests who were excluded from the decision-making body. Although a single trade policy-making body headed Korea's FTAs, opposition from protectionist ministries continued to hamper MOFAT's ability to efficiently pursue FTAs. For example, opposition from the Ministry of Agriculture and the Ministry of Culture and Tourism led to long delays and stalemates in the Korea-Chile FTA negotiations and Korea's Bilateral Investment Treaty with the United States.

Policy coordination mechanism through the Ministerial Meeting on External Economic Affairs was also instrumental in advancing national interests ahead of sectoral interests. Through consensus building based on discussion, the Ministerial Meetings had the effect of moderating opposition voices to trade liberalization. Korea's cohesive domestic trade governance was instrumental in securing Korea's comprehensive and high-level FTA with the US and the EU. During Korea's FTA negotiation with the US, MOFAT was able to pursue greater agricultural liberalization in order to gain a general access to the US market and thus secure national economic benefits despite strong domestic opposition.

Japan: Fragmented Trade Governance

Japan lacked a cohesive and centralized trade policy-making structure, compared to Korea. Representatives from Ministry of Foreign Affairs (MOFA), Ministry of Finance, and Ministry of Economy, Trade, and Industry (METI) have traditionally dominated trade negotiations for items under their jurisdiction. These representatives have essentially acted as independent negotiators serving the interests of their ministries. As a result, Japan's counterparts in trade negotiations often faced several equally powerful ministries with different interests.

By enabling any single ministry among the three key ministries to serve as a veto player, Japan's domestic trade governance strengthened the voice of sectoral interests, specifically protectionist interests in trade policy-making. This, in turn, highly limited the nature and type of Japan's trade negotiations. Due to this fragmented trade governance, Japan was only able to sign FTAs with small trade partners that did not threaten its agricultural sector during the first decade of the 21st century.

In fact, Japan's trade policy-making structure was not static throughout this time period. Under reform-minded Japanese Prime Minister Junichiro Koizumi's administration, efforts were made to bolster centralization and coordination in the policy-making structure. Similarly, when the Democratic Party of Japan (DPJ) assumed control of the government in 2009, it also tried to centralize the authority over trade negotiations at the cabinet level to weaken ministerial interests. These efforts, however, fell short of creating an independent body that would head trade policies and override ministerial divisions. Ministries such as the Ministry of Agriculture, Forestry, and Fisheries (MAFF) that opposed FTAs and trade liberalization continued to remain as key veto players in Japan's trade policy-making process.

Table 7. Trade Governance between Korea and Japan

Domestic Trade Governance		
Characteristics of FTAs	**Cohesive**	**Fragmented**
High-level FTA (comprehensive liberalization)	Korea (1998–2012) *Japan (post-2013)**	
Low-level FTA (protectionist)		Japan (1990–2012) *Korea (post-2013)**

Trade governance is cohesive when sectoral interests are effectively coordinated under national interests, and fragmented when sectoral interests dominate at the expense of national interest.
There is strong correlation between cohesiveness of trade governance and depth of FTA. Cohesive trade governance is more likely to be associated with high-level FTA, while fragmented trade governance is more likely to be associated with low-level FT.
In the first decade of the 21st century, Korea's cohesive trade governance led to high-level FTA, and Japan's fragmented trade governance led to low-level FTA.

**Source: Choi and Oh (2011)

Japan in the Lost Decades

Since the early 1990s, Japan has been mired in the Lost Decades. The second largest economy in the world, which was challenging the number one status of the American economy in the 1980s, was somehow caught in a trap. Keynesian macro policies proved ineffective. A Lost Decade, which started with the burst of bubble in 1990, was becoming Lost Decades. Experts called for reform to spur productivity and remove inefficiency. Unstable political leadership failed to implement reform. Hence, most reform initiatives remained at the drawing board. The Japanese economy was barely breathing. Demographics played a certain role in the process. The most rapidly aging society with the highest longevity in the world meant lowering demand for consumption. Old Japanese were extremely careful in their spending decisions, because they knew they were facing a long life after retirement without steady sources of income and weak social safety net. They did not respond to the virtually negative interest rate, as expected by policy makers.

What went wrong? Clues might be found in ICT. The 1990s were the great time of technological breakthrough. The wave of "C&C" (Computer and Communication) and digital technology swept the global economic landscape. For the first time in human history, everyone could afford her own telephone number, and the internet was used as a communication platform. It gave rise to the death of distance. Communication cost became exponentially cheaper. In particular, international telephone call fees became incredibly low. Firms were swiftly adjusting to the rising tide of the C&C. The entire production process from R&D, design, procuring parts and components, assembly, distribution, marketing, and after-sale service became fragmented and relocated throughout the global village. Communication revolution enabled business activities conducted in different time zones to get integrated. The nature of international trade became fundamentally different. The text book concept of trade as "make a product all in country A and ship to country B" needed not be the one and only mode of trade. Various segments or tasks in the production stage could be shipped to foreign countries from the firm's headquarter country.

While the business sector was busy making the most of ICT, policy makers were grappling to figure out a proper policy toward ICT. ICT was seen as a double-edged sword. New opportunities for new industries, new organizations, new life styles, and much more were on the horizon. Standards were critical aspect of ICT. Without common standards, communication would be isolated within a few people. In the markets, several standards were competing. Since it was only the beginning, none of them were dominant. There was no commonly agreed procedure to adopt a particular standard. Without government intervention, the market would decide the outcome. Different countries adopted different approaches. The US resorted to the market-based approach. Whichever standard emerges from the market, it would become the de facto standard, as long as the market competition was fair. From this perspective, the role of the government was to ensure no abuse of the market power by big players.

Unlike the US, the EU relied on the committee and consensus approach. The committee would review various standards and try to develop a consensus on the particular standard. Such an approach amply reflected the spirit of the EU. The EU had evolved into the economic union in a strict sense: free flow of products, services, investment, and ideas. A single pan-European standard would facilitate the seamless flow of product, service, investments, and ideas across national borders. The EU approach is distinctively an active industrial policy, whereas the US approach is far from government intervention. The global trading sysem did not have any rules on this matter.

Back in the 1990s, the choice of Japan in ICT standards was to come up with unique Japanese standards, which would be incompatible with other standards. Japanese policy makers wanted to keep their domestic market from foreign technology and products. Based on the sheer strength of the Japanese electronics industry, Japan wanted to protect its second largest economy. In retrospect, such a policy decision kept the Japanese economy at bay. Inward-looking industrial policy in ICT hampered the chance for Japan to get out of long depression.

China: Moving from the WTO to the FTA

China was aware of the importance of securing trade preference for its products in the global market. Securing a seat at the WTO was not sufficient. Right after joining the WTO, China began to negotiate FTAs. China's approach to FTAs was rather pragmatic.

In the beginning phase, China focused on tariff reduction in goods. Its negotiation agenda did not cover service and investments. Even with goods, China did not aim for tariff elimination in principle. Compared with the negotiation approach by the US and the EU, which adopted in principle "complete tariff elimination with a very few exceptions," China's approach reflected its level of economic development. While China was anxious to enhance market access, it was equally concerned about the protection of domestic import-competing sectors. China had protectionist-bias. Even though it pursued actively the expansion of bilateral FTA network, China did not aim for substantial opening up of the Chinese market. In finding FTA partners, China eyed on the sphere of the Chinese diaspora. ASEAN was approached and negotiated with for an FTA.

Compared to Korea and Japan, domestic trade governance becomes a lesser issue in the case of China. As a regime with one party without periodic popular elections, China does not have domestic contest for leadership in trade policy as openly and transparently as Korea and Japan have. Without doubt, such a battle would take place. However, coordination mechanisms and the process of exerting influence by non-governmental sectors are secretive.

6. Strategic Effect of the KORUS in Northeast Asia

As the KORUS FTA became a real possibility, concerns over trade diversion effects prompted major players, such as China and the EU, to express strong interests in FTA talks with Korea. Likewise, the Japanese government raised the prospect of resuming the Korea-Japan FTA talks which had been suspended since 2004. Among those countries, the EU was Korea's first choice. Negotiations with China and Japan were set aside for the time being. Korea's decision to negotiate with the EU was a strategy to press the US in the Korea-US FTA talks. The Korean market was severely contested by the American and the European agriculture, automobile, and pharmaceuticals industry, and also professional services like accounting, consulting, legal service, educations, and financial services. The Korean government played the principle of parity to the US and the EU in terms of trade liberalization. As it turns out, the US and the EU alike played the principle of parity as their negotiating tactic. As a result, the KORUS and the Korea-EU FTA achieved in-depth trade liberalization.

The resumption of the Korea-Japan FTA talks was not easy. Despite renewed urgency for the case, mainly due to the Japanese concern of trade diversion, the already-identified obstacles, which helped cause the breakdown of earlier bilateral negotiations in 2003-2004, still proved to be obstacles. Japan could not come up with an upgraded version of the agriculture sector opening and its negotiation stance on non-tariff measures (NTM). The Japanese business sector became quite concerned about the negative effects, especially from the Korea-EU.[28] Compared to Korea, leadership and domestic trade governance in Japan were not forthcoming to stand up to the challenges.

Run-up to the Korea-China FTA talks was also not smooth for Beijing. It was no secret that Beijing was anxious to get even with the US by having the Korea-China FTA. Seoul was divided between pros and cons. Korea's economic case for the Korea-China FTA was mainly based on trade preemption. In order to capture a sizable market share in the growing Chinese consumer market, the Korea-China FTA was essential, according to the protagonists. The case against the Korea-China FTA was built on the

28 Yoshimatsu (2015)

plight of the farming sector: the Korea-China FTA would create more adverse challenges to Korean farmers due to geographic proximity. To tilt the balance, a political case for an FTA between Korea and China was strongly argued by some. To gain leverage in the inter-Korean relations, the argument went on, Beijing would be less keen to stand for Pyongyang's interests, if commercial ties between Korea and China get intensified through an FTA. Such non-economic argument invited a strong counter argument, saying that Beijing would never give up North Korea. North Korean military provocations in 2010 and China straddling the fence to the dismay of the engagement circle in Seoul inevitably prompted further delay for launching the Korea-China FTA talks.

7. Appraisal and Summary

In the first decade of the 21st century, countries in the Northeast Asia were mindful of creating their own strategic advantage through bilateral FTA. What has occurred in the first decade of the new millennium in the Northeast Asia trade architecture is summarized and assessed as follows:

1. With China's membership in the WTO, Northeast Asia at last secured the basic institutional backup for trade relations.

2. Japan and Korea demanded more investment liberalization and protection to China. Korea, Japan, and China agreed on the necessity of more institutionalization on investment rule, but the steps to establish such a rule were incremental and slow. They were afraid of domestic opposition.

The agriculture sector was holding the key.

3. Instead of directly taking up the CJK FTA, Korea, Japan, and China moved to develop its own respective FTA networks, not involving the others. In the early stage, all three were negotiating with small and medium-sized economies, where agriculture was not a focal point of liberalization. The process of building FTA networks was slow.

4. The Korea-Japan FTA negotiations were the first bilateral FTA attempted in Northeast Asia. Only after a year of talks, negotiation efforts collapsed. Japan's reluctance in liberalizing agriculture sector was most blamable.

5. Change in the race came when Korea decided to negotiate an FTA with the US. Considering the agriculture sector opposition and strong anti-American sentiment, the idea of Korea proposing an FTA to the US was out of the blue. The left-wing Korean government adopted a right-wing trade policy.

6. Korea became most active and bold in FTA network building. It negotiated FTAs with the US and the EU - the two biggest economies in the world. Since Korean and Japanese firms were competing head-to-head in those markets, pressure was mounting on the Japanese government to counter trade disadvantages.

7. By the end of 2010, Northeast Asia had not evolved much further from the beginning of the century. There was no bilateral FTA in any pair among Korea, Japan, and China. Instead, each country tried to preempt the other by a series of bilateral FTAs with other countries. In terms of scope and

coverage, Korea was ahead of the game.

8. While further institutionalization in Northeast Asia failed to materialize, it is noteworthy that Korea, Japan, and China respectively negotiated FTAs with ASEAN. The fear of trade diversion drove such an 'ASEAN + 1' outcome.

4 Trade Architecture Competition in the 2010s

1. In Search of a Platform for Deep Integration

At the dawn of the second decade of the 21st century, Northeast Asia did not have any additional institutions beyond the WTO. As analyzed in the preceding chapter, during the first decade of the new millennium, the three countries allocated more political assets and negotiating resources to edge out the other neighbors with the aim of creating a trade preemption effect. The only bilateral FTA talks among the three countries were between Korea and Japan. After a year-long negotiation, the talks were suspended. Each side came to the assessment that the other side was not primed for high-level liberalization. The Korean negotiators were frustrated about Japan's unwillingness to offer a substantial part of agricultural farming products and to negotiate NTMs. The Japanese negotiators found strong opposition from the Korean auto sector and small and medium-sized firms. Despite strong and persistent requests from China, Korea could not determine whether to go ahead with the idea of the Korea-China FTA.

Korea had strong doubts about China's seriousness in opening up the service sector and upgrading investment policy. Under this backdrop, negotiating a full-blown CJK FTA was a non-starter. As a backup plan, Korea, Japan, and China agreed to negotiate the trilateral investment agreement, building on their existing bilateral BITs.

Another significant development was the failure to complete the DDA negotiations under the aegis of the WTO. When the DDA was launched, the negotiators aimed to complete the talks by 2004. While not many took the deadline seriously (major trade negotiations had the habit of missing the deadline), not many neither predicted the DDA would continue into the next decade. After 2006, the DDA talks were virtually suspended. What was alarming to free traders was the lack of progress. DDA negotiations moved between official suspension and virtual suspension. Several factors contributed to the stalemate of DDA negotiations. Lack of US leadership and the politicized nature of the WTO process, among others, were to be blamed. Visibly, the US was turning to bilateral and regional trade agreements as alternatives. Delayed DDA and changing trade strategy of the US presented another strong case for Korea, Japan, and China to come up with plan B for securing and enhancing market access.

Emergence of TPP

While the frontal attack on the CJK FTA was off from strategy map of Seoul, Tokyo, and Beijing, roundabout routes were considered and sought. ASEAN emerged as a focal point in the process. ASEAN has an FTA each with China, Japan, and Korea. A natural suggestion was to integrate the three "ASEAN + 1" agreement into a single framework. Beijing began to circulate this idea, naming it as "ASEAN + 3." Tokyo was not quite comfortable with such a formulation. In particular, Tokyo was concerned about the China-centric aspect behind ASEAN + 3. As a counter measure, Tokyo came up with the idea of "ASEAN + 6," where Australia, New Zealand, and India would join the platform of ASEAN + 3. By bringing those countries, Tokyo thought the China-centric element would be mitigated. To the eyes of policy makers in Tokyo, those three countries were strong allies of Japan and often found themselves disagreeing with China on foreign policy issues.

Due to sharp differences between Beijing and Tokyo, launching Asia region-wide trade negotiations was being delayed. What had promoted Beijing and Tokyo to make a compromise was what was happening on the other side of the Pacific. Towards the end of the Bush administration, the US joined a small group of 4 countries - New Zealand, Chile, Singapore, and Brunei - and turned the negotiations into Trans Pacific Partnership (TPP). Before long, Australia, Canada, and Mexico joined the talks. Some ASEAN members like Vietnam and Malaysia also decided to join the TPP talks. The US marketed the TPP as a mega FTA, which would set new trade rules for the 21st century. The idea of creating such a new mega FTA seemed attractive, due to a virtual impasse for the DDA. Under US leadership, the momentum was building. By the end of 2012, the number of countries engaging in TPP negotiations increased to 11.

RCEP as a competitor

A notable absence was China, Japan, and Korea. Each country was not joining the TPP talks for different reasons. China found the ambitious negotiating agenda of the TPP hard to accept. Washington pressed hard to negotiate issues sensitive to China, including State-Owned Enterprise (SOE), Labor, Environment, ISDS, and so on. Realizing the height of hurdles, China started to accuse the TPP as a China-containing conspiracy. Japan had been internally discussing its membership at the TPP for some time. Since it could not effectively deal with the stubborn resistance from its agricultural sector, Japan remained indecisive. As for Korea, the sense of complacency crept in. Korea thought it was ahead of the game of trade preemption vis-à-vis Japan and China, because neither China for Japan had an FTA with the US nor with the EU, while Korea had clinched an FTA with the US and with the EU. Seoul downplayed the significance of a mega FTA.

Snowballing expansion of TPP membership led ASEAN to propose the ASEAN + 6 platform to China and Japan as its alternative. The proposal had its own rationale. Each of the six non-ASEAN countries (Korea, Japan, China, Australia, New Zealand, and India) had its bilateral FTA with ASEAN. In November 2012, the 16 countries announced to launch the Regional Comprehensive Economic Partnership (RCEP). Interestingly, China, Japan, and Korea announced the launching of their trilateral FTA (CJK FTA) on the same day and in the same place. After a decade of joint studies at various levels, the CJK FTA talks got launched at last. Hence, the stage is set for a race among TPP, RCEP, and CJK FTA.

2. TPP: US-Japan Alliance

What drove the US to the initiative of the TPP? One needs to take note of the timing of the US decision to launch TPP talks. It was 2008, the year when the Global Financial Crisis broke out from the US. The Financial Crisis prompted Chinese top elites to challenge the US hegemony in the global economic architecture, which in turn propelled the US to respond. Realizing ineffectiveness of the conventional approach to China, the US came to the conclusion of inventing a different grand strategy of confrontation. The strategic shift started with President Obama. The Obama administration assessed that the US projected too much power and resources in the Middle East, compared to East Asia. It also realized the urgency of addressing the assertive China. Otherwise, power in East Asia may shift decisively away from America to China. Hence, the strategy of "rebalancing to Asia" had emerged.[29]

Rebalancing to Asia had two main policy tools. Military balancing against China through a shift in deployments and new arrangements with allies such as Japan and the Philippines was one. The other was to push the 21st century regional trade initiative. The TPP had been sold publicly as an attempt to achieve the second policy. The naming of the TPP may be misleading. At first glance, people would not have a clear idea of what it means and what

29 Since 2011 when US Secretary of State Hillary Clinton announced the US "pivot" to Asia, it has been enshrined as a central focus of U.S. foreign policy.

it tries to achieve. In fact, the TPP is a trade agreement in the Asia-Pacific region. Negotiators aimed to create trade rules relating to the new landscape of the global economy, which are not covered by the WTO. They wanted to create TPP in the vast region of the Asia-Pacific. The TPP, however, was not just a typical trade agreement. Strategic dimensions of the TPP was in full display when Obama said in his last State of Union address (January 2016): "With TPP, China does not set the rules in that region; we do."

Japan joins the TPP talks: Game-Changing Move

When Japan finally decided to join the TPP talks in early 2013 after years of indecisiveness, the TPP talks became the most significant trade negotiations on the planet. With Japan on board, the TPP negotiations enjoyed global attention. Never before did Japan join such a high profile and high stake FTA negotiations.

In the midst of global wave of FTA race in the early 21st century, Japan had not had any meaningful FTAs with any major country, due to political risks of the agricultural market opening. For this unbearable risk, no Japanese government had the idea of pursuing FTAs with the US and the EU. Japan stood in the sideline with the sense of being left out in the cold, when Korea was actively pursuing an FTA with the US and with the EU. For Japanese firms competing with Korean firms in the US and the EU, the advance of Korea meant the negative effect of trade diversion. Pressures were built to get even with Korea. The TPP presented a golden opportunity for Japan to get even with Korea.

To the eyes of the Japanese, the TPP was the Second Black Ship. The Black Ship (Kurofune) of Commodore Perry, which arrived in the bay of Tokyo in 1853, forced the grand opening of Japan from two hundred years of seclusion from the world. As the First Black Ship woke the Japanese from isolation from the global trends toward its own path of development, the Second Black Ship is expected to take them to another path of development. So far, Japan has been trapped in the Lost Decades. Nonetheless, leadership of Japan could not decide to swallow hard and welcome the Second Black Ship. After a long hesitation, Japan decided to move forward. Japan indicated interest in the TPP publicly at APEC in 2011, when Japanese Prime Minister Noda announced Japan's interest in the TPP negotiations. Almost two years of internal deliberation and consultation with the other TPP participants were required before Japan's formal announcement of joining the TPP talks. It was timed with the declaration of Prime Minister Abe's bold assertion: "Japan is back."

What has led the reluctant Japan to embrace the bold idea of "the Second Grand Opening?" It is the combination of economic strategy and political strategy. Shinzo Abe, the Japanese Prime Minister, who came to power in the final month of 2012, unveiled a bold economic blue print for the revitalization of Japan, dubbed as Abenomics. Japan had been suffering from the Lost Decades since the burst of bubble in 1990. During these two decades, Japan virtually ceased to grow. The Japanese economy, which was rapidly growing and threatened the number one status of the US economy, all of sudden got trapped in prolonged depression.

Abenomics had three elements: aggressive monetary expansion, fiscal expansion, and structural reform. The Intention of expansionary macro policy was to upend the Japanese people's mindset of "depression": "We should not spend, because the winter will be long and harsh. Instead, we should save and save for the future." During the Lost Decades, real interest rate was close to zero or sometimes even negative. However, such a low interest rate did not bring more investment, or more consumption of durable goods like auto and housing, usually based on loans. Abenomics set the goal of an inflation rate of 2 percent. Engineering toward the path of mild inflation would change people's spending decisions. With increased spending, more investments would be made. Through this process, deflationary psychology would be replaced with a virtuous circle of consumption-investment-more consumption. Revitalization should not be short-lived. Hence, a new engine for growth was in need. Structural reform and deregulation were considered to be instrumental. Japan joining the TPP was decided in this context. Nonetheless, economic strategy alone cannot account for Abe's decision to join the TPP negotiations. When it comes to the economic effect of TPP, previous administrations before Abe must have thought in a similar manner. They have been hesitant to join the talks. Then why was Abe different?

"Japan is Back" vs "Rise of Assertive China"

Japan was increasingly uncomfortable with the rise of assertive China. When China became a member of the G20 Summit in 2008, Japan became nervous because it could not solely represent the interests of Asia any more in a prestigious global economic club. The G20 Summit provided a venue for China to voice up its demand for changing global economic governance. The G20 agreement on transferring more equity position to China from European countries, albeit a small percentage, was symbolic.

The rise of China was making contrasts with the limits of Japan in the global stage. When Japan circulated the idea of the Asian Monetary Fund (AMF) in the wake of the 1997 Asian Financial Crisis, it was blocked by the US. When China circulated the initiative of creating the Asian Infrastructure Investment Bank (AIIB) in 2014, eventually the idea overcame a strong opposition by the US and became a reality.

When the term G2 was first circulated to the public stage, the expression was not well received in China. Power elites in China took the G2 as a US tactic to request more burden-sharing on global affairs on their country. The initial response was "We are still a developing country. We have so many burning domestic issues to deal with." This kind of response was very much in line with the admonition of Deng Xiaping's "bide your time, hide your brightness." However, lukewarm response to the idea of G2 did not last that long.

From the early years of the 2010s, China was getting bolder and more ambitious in the global stage. To the eyes of the Japanese, China was not only rapidly rising, but also increasingly assertive. Japan was in dire necessity of a strategy to deal with China. The territorial dispute over Shenkaku islands, which the Chinese call Diaoyu Islands, during 2012-2013 was so alarming to Japan. China's growing confrontational approach in the South China Sea dispute doubled the imminent danger of assertive China to Japan.

When Abe came to power in late 2012, he had two things in mind: creating a blueprint to revitalize Japan, and a strategy to deal with the assertive China. Revitalization of Japan and standing up to the assertive China were connected through the TPP. In his first visit to the US in 2013 as Prime Minister, Abe declared "Japan is back." The political grip of the Japanese ruling party had not been strong. It was almost an annual event of selecting a new Prime Minister. In Japan, the joke was that people could not remember the name of their Prime Minister, because the incumbent got replaced after a fleetingly short time. It was critical to maintain power to exert any influence.

From the US point of view, the Rebalancing to Asia strategy would work better if a reliable and strong partner could be found. Japan would be a perfect candidate. Hence, when Japan decided to join the TPP negotiations, the US-Japan alliance was made. During his visit to the US in April 2015, Abe delivered a speech at the Congress. As a matter of fact, his speech at the Joint Session of Congress (Both Senate and House) was the first time for a Japanese Prime Minister. During his speech at the US Congress, Prime Minister Abe said on the TPP:

> *"Involving countries in Asia-Pacific whose backgrounds vary, the U.S. and Japan must take the lead. We must take the lead to build a market that is fair, dynamic, sustainable, and is also free from the arbitrary intentions of any nation.*
>
> *In the Pacific market, we cannot overlook sweat shops or burdens on the*

environment. Nor can we simply allow free riders on intellectual property. No. Instead, we can spread our shared values around the world and have them take root: the rule of law, democracy, and freedom. That is exactly what the TPP is all about.

Furthermore, the TPP goes far beyond just economic benefits. It is also about our security."[30]

Abe's remarks vividly illustrated what Japan intended in order to deal with the rise of assertive China. When Abe mentions "environment" and "intellectual property," he was mindful of the assertive China. Reference to rule of law, democracy, and freedom was also mindful of China. To the mindset of the Japanese power elites, the TPP was, in essence, the US-Japan economic and security alliance.

The heads of the US and Japan spent their political capital to make progress in the TPP and complete the negotiations as soon as possible. Japan's decision to join the TPP was a game-changing move. When Korea was vigorously pursuing FTAs with the US and the EU in the first decade of the new millennium, Japan was not able to emulate the success of Korea. Even though Japan had been contemplating its participation at the TPP talks for some time, the decisive leadership of Prime Minister Abe was instrumental in Japan's place at the TPP. Abe's decision to join the TPP negotiations was propelled by the significance of economic reform under

30 Abe (2015). "Toward an Alliance of Hope" was the title of his speech.

the economic blueprint of Abenomics and strategic vision of consolidating the US-Japan alliance in order to contain the rise of China. Never before had Japan committed to comprehensive tariff cut in this scale and scope.

Japan in TPP: the Greatest Agricultural Concession[31]

When the TPP negotiations were concluded, Japan agreed to "greatest agricultural concessions Japan has made in the history of trade negotiations ."[32] Japan's tariff concessions covered 81 percent of its agricultural products, including immediate tariff elimination on nearly half of the agricultural products. Out of the 586 items categorized as sensitive products, tariffs were eliminated for 174 items (about 30 percent). For the remaining 412 items, the Japanese government agreed to tariff reductions and import quota expansions. For example, beef tariffs will be lowered immediately from 38.5 percent to 27.5 percent, and then further reduce to 9 percent over the span of 16 years. The 4.3 percent tariffs on high-priced pork will be abolished in ten years and the 482 yen/kg tariffs on low-priced pork will fall to 50 yen/kg in the same period. The Japanese government also agreed to eliminate and/or reduce tariffs on many of its dairy products (e.g., cheddar, gouda, cream cheese, ice cream, yogurt, and whole milk powder) whose tariffs range up to 40 percent. Japan's agricultural tariff concessions fall short when compared to other TPP member states that have agreed to abolish tariffs on over 90

---

31 Discussion in this part borrows from Choi and Oh (2017).

32 Takashi (2015)

percent of their agricultural products. Nonetheless, the TPP marks Japan's greatest agricultural liberalization where most of its vegetables, fruits, and fishery products and a third of its sensitive products will become tariff free in a decade or so.

Considering strong opposition from the farm lobby and organized interests in politics, such an outcome is remarkable. Leadership, strategy, and domestic trade governance played an instrumental role. The Japanese government entered the TPP negotiations with a highly defensive position on agricultural liberalization, reflecting the strong domestic political concern towards TPP's impact on agricultural liberalization. In the early stage of negotiations, the Diet of Japan had passed a resolution opposing liberalization of the five sensitive agricultural products - rice, wheat and barley, beef and pork, dairy products, sugar and starch crops - and demanded that they should be either excluded from the negotiations or negotiated for special measures to ensure sustainable domestic production. "Even the gradual elimination of tariffs over a period of more than ten years is unacceptable," they declared.[33] Japan participated in the TPP only after President Barak Obama confirmed that Japan "is not required to make a prior commitment to unilaterally eliminate all tariffs upon joining the TPP negotiations."[34]

---

33 House of Councillors, The National Diet of Japan, "Resolution on Japan's Participation in the Trans-Pacific Partnership (TPP) Negotiations" (April 2013)

34 Prime Minister of Japan and his Cabinet, "Press Conference by Prime Minister Shinzo

By designing a negotiating taskforce in a manner that the sectoral interest of agriculture would be less powerful, and also by reforming the organization for the farm lobby, Prime Minister Abe dealt with tough political battle from both his ruling party and the opposition party. Abe appointed "well-known advocates of free trade" for the agriculture minister. So under Prime Minister Abe's administration, agriculture ministers supported TPP even at the cost of reforming and liberalizing Japan's heavily protected agricultural sector. Through those maneuvers, the institution in charge of Japan's TPP was highly unfavorable to agricultural interests. Abe's strategy was to weaken the veto power of the agriculture ministry in TPP negotiations. Prime Minister Abe directly targeted Japan's powerful farm lobby, the Central Union of Agricultural Cooperatives (JA-Zenchu), for structural reform in order to push forward the TPP negotiations.

Korea's Hesitance in Joining TPP[35]

When the conclusion of the TPP was reached on October 2015, Korea was absent. The Korean government came under immediate fire. How come Korea did not join the TPP?

Prior to Japan's entry into the TPP talks, Korea did not take TPP seriously. With FTAs with the largest economy in the world, the US, and the EU, and preparatory works to launch FTA negotiations with China,

Abe during His Visit to the United States of America," (February 2013)

35 Discussion in this part draws on Choi and Oh (2017).

the Korean government felt it "had enough on its plate." Korea's position is understandable because the TPP was not moving forward, and the US did not have fast track authority. Yet, Korea's position on the TPP should have changed when Japan joined the TPP negotiations in 2013.

Korea and Japan have similar trade structures - Korean and Japanese firms use their factories in Southeast Asian countries as manufacturing bases to export to the United States. Japan, as a member of the TPP, can capitalize on the supply chain of origin with other TPP members in Southeast Asia to further expand its export market. Korea is bound to be disadvantaged if it relies mainly on FTAs. In April 2013, the United States once again encouraged Korea to join the TPP, but Korea remained indecisive.

Korea's hesitance in joining the TPP negotiations stems from sectoral interests that oppose a free trade pact with Japan. One of the largest opponents to Korea joining the TPP came from Korean automakers who feared that Japanese automobiles would flood the Korean market while Korean companies could sell virtually none in the Japanese market. Foreign share in the Japanese auto market is six percent - the lowest among OECD member states – and the share of Korean auto is virtually nil. At the public hearing on Korea's participation in the TPP, the Korean auto sector made a public complaint about its disadvantage vis-à-vis Japanese counterparts.

The Korean government was heavily influenced by the sectoral interest at the cost of national interest. After a year-long hesitance, Korea came to the conclusion that it would not join the TPP negotiations, by announcing that the Korea-China FTA was the top priority over the TPP.

3. Race between TPP and RCEP[36]

The global economy has taken a new landscape, driven by technological advances and digital revolution. Deepening the GVC, vibrant cross-border flow of capital and digital trade have become an integral part of the global economy, but not effectively reflected in the current global trading rule. As for investment, various bilateral investment treaties have been agreed but failed to form a multilateral investment agreement. Considering the ever-increasing flow of cross-border investment, the patchwork of bilateral ties would generate regulatory confusion and risk to investors and regulatory loophole for policymakers. In the light of neck-breaking speed of digital transaction across national borders, the absence of trading rule in this new economy is striking.

If this gap between economic realities and trade disciplines persists, it would create regulatory uncertainty and risk, with the likely impact of only strengthening the dominance of incumbents at the expense of innovation and consumers. While the WTO has not delivered any meaningful response to this task of the times,[37] like-minded countries aim to establish trade rule in these areas amongst themselves before others do. This is essentially the

---

36 This section heavily draws on Choi (2016).

37 At the WTO Ministerial Conference in Nairobi 2015, the US made it public that the Doha Round (formally, known as the Doha Development Agenda) had reached the dead end. (Froman, 2015; USTR, 2015)

nature of the competition between the TPP and the RCEP.

RCEP has been negotiated since 2012 among 16 countries: 10 member states of ASEAN and 6 states, each of which has an FTA with ASEAN (under the form of ASEAN + 1). Negotiations for the RCEP have been slow. When the TPP talks were fast-moving, the RCEP talks had a target to chase. In terms of the negotiating agenda, the TPP and the RCEP have common elements in Market access for goods (TPP aimed at 100%, RCEP aimed for 90%), Rules of origin, Trade facilitation, Services (TPP adopted a "negative list," RCEP adopted a "positive list"), Investment, Competition, Intellectual Property, and Development. There are a wide range of issues included only in the TPP, and not in the RCEP. These are Government Procurement, SOE, E-Commerce, Environment, Labour, Trade Remedies, Textiles and Apparel, Temporary Entry, Horizontal Issues like Small and Medium-sized Enterprise (SME), Supply Chain Facilitation, and Regulatory Coherence. These issues exclusive to the TPP are often called "21st Century Issues." Considering its negotiations agenda, comparison with the RCEP, and achievement, the TPP is a "high standard," "21st century," and "comprehensive" agreement.

Table 8. TPP and RCEP: Common Elements and Differences in Agenda

Common Elements	TPP Only
Market access for goods 'TPP' aimed at 100%, RCEP aiming for 90%	Government Procurement
Rules of origin	SOEs unless included in RCEP under Competition
Trade facilitation? Customs Sanitary and Phytosanitary measures and agreement (SPS) Technical Barriers to Trade (TBT)	E-Commerce
Services TPP adopted "negative list", RCEP adopted "positive list"	Environment
Investment	Labour
Competition	Trade Remedies
Intellectual Property	Textiles and Apparel
Development Horizontal issue in TPP	Temporary Entry
Dispute Settlement	Horizontal Issues SMEs Supply Chain Facilitation Regulatory Coherence
"Other Issues" (RCEP)	Separate Chapters in TPP Telecommunications Financial Services

**Source: Scollay (2016), USTR(2016)

In terms of economic significance, the membership of the TPP covers 37.4% of the global GDP (Gross Domestic Product) and 27% of the world trade, while 30.6% of the global GDP and 30.2% of the world trade is covered by the members in the RCEP.[38] These mega FTAs build on the decade-long attempt of making bilateral FTAs in East Asia. While the motivation of harmonizing and integrating a variety of rules of origins in bilateral FTAs has given rise to the necessity for a mega FTA, these mega FTAs aim further and beyond the familiar work program of a bilateral FTA: substantial liberalization of service and investment, introduction of disciplines on behind-the-border measures, and establishment of trading rules related to the digital economy. Through a series of multilateral negotiations under the aegis of the GATT in the 20th century and a series of bilateral FTAs in the early part of the 21st century, tariffs on goods have been reduced to a substantially low level in many East Asian countries. When tariffs become a "trade issue," it is mainly for two reasons: first, the gap between binding tariffs and actual ones is large, hence creating uncertainty for trading partners; second, the remaining binding tariffs are difficult to be reduced due to stubborn domestic opposition. For these reasons, the importance of tariff negotiations is not the same as before. Tariff negotiations are no longer the most important negotiating agenda for trade talks. This is precisely the case in the TPP and the RCEP.

TPP ahead of RCEP

TPP talks came to a conclusion in October 2015. The 12 countries of the TPP signed on the agreement in February 2016. On the other hand, RCEP talks were still under way without making headway towards completion. In the competition for establishing trading rule, the TPP was

---

38 Trade data is based on IMF(2014), and GDP data is based on IMF(2015).

clearly ahead of the game. With the last step of domestic ratification, the TPP would go into effect. On the other hand, the RCEP had been slow in moving. By then, the 16 participating countries had 16 rounds of talks with a modest progress. They agreed to delay the deadline to the end of 2016. Notwithstanding this asymmetry in progress, "the last step" in making the TPP as a reality proved to be an uphill battle. As the next course of history tells, the TPP could not survive the domestic scrutiny of the US. When the TPP was signed and was ready for its final step before entry into force, ratification by the US Congress was a critical step. The TPP agreement was structured to the manner that the TPP would not be effective without the US.

According to the TPP agreement, it will enter into force 60 days after all original signatories have notified completion of their domestic legal procedures. If this has not occurred within two years of signature, the Agreement will enter into force 60 days after the expiry of that two year period if at least six original signatories accounting for 85 percent of the combined GDP of the original signatories have ratified the agreement.[39] Even if all other 11 signatories complete their ratification process, the TPP would not be effective without US ratification.[40]

39 Article 30.5 "Entry into Force" in Chapter 30 "Final Provisions" from the TPP Agreement. (USTR, 2016)

40 Among the 12 signatories, the US has 62% and Japan has 17% of the GDP share. Hence, the TPP will not become effective without ratification from both the US and Japan, if the 85% threshold is to be invoked. It would be unimaginable for Japan to

Seeking ratification in the US Congress was a race against the time. When the TPP was signed by the 12 negotiating countries, it was February 2016. The US Presidential election was to take place in November. Election was only several months away. US politics was already overtaken by the heat of the election. Sentiments were running against the TPP. The TPP agreement was not welcomed by those key politicians who supported the TPP before because of disappointing agreements of their focus. Without fixing those problems, they vowed not to approve the deal. It was getting worse. None of the major Presidential candidates were supportive of the TPP. Trump, who was seeking candidacy at the Republican Party, and Sanders, a popular politician from the Democratic Party, were critical of the TPP, accusing it as race to the bottom. Hillary, a promising candidate looking for her nomination at the Democratic Party, who served as the Secretary of the State for President Obama and supported the TPP as a critical element of the Rebalancing to Asia strategy, changed her stance on the TPP as well. Strong headwind of protectionism was blowing strong in the US.

President Obama, whose vision and gut carried the TPP to conclusion, was counting his days in office. While the Obama administration was adamant in pushing the TPP during the lame-duck session, his chance of getting ratification was slim. During the summer of 2016, many speculation and projection were offered about the prospect of obtaining ratification of

reject the TPP, once the US ratifies it.

the TPP. Some argued that the lame-duck session after the election would be a window of opportunity, and the Congress might grudgingly ratify it in case of Hillary's win of the Presidential election. In his analysis of the TPP ratification in the US, Choi (2016) argued that such a projection would be wishful thinking, and the ratification would be delayed for a while. Choi's logic was based on two factors: history and sentiment. No major treaty has ever been ratified at the lame-duck Congress. Moreover, intellectual support for the TPP was shadowed by the rising tide of anti-globalization and protectionism.

4. TPP without the US

With the victory of Trump, the possibility of ratification at the lame-duck session disappeared like mist in the spring. Trump rose from a minor outsider to the Presidential candidate of the Republican Party. In his remarkable rise, his destructive anti-trade and anti-global speeches and stances played a great role. Trump claimed:

> *"Globalization has made the financial elite, who donate to politicians, very wealthy. …But it has left millions of our workers with nothing but poverty and heartache. …Trillions of our dollars and millions of our jobs flowed overseas. …Today, we import nearly [US]$800 billion more in goods than we export. We can't continue to do that."*[41]

Trump also lambasted trade agreements:

> *"[First], the disaster called NAFTA. Second, China's entry into the WTO. And finally, 'The Trans-Pacific Partnership is the greatest danger yet. The TPP, as it is known, would be the death blow for American manufacturing."*[42]

Trump's anti-trade stance is a radical departure from the conventional Republican Party stance on trade. The past Republican presidents have negotiated the Uruguay Round, the NAFTA, and the KORUS FTA. His predecessors maintained a pro-trade stance in the middle of controversies. Trump appeals to those distressed by import competition by accusing past trade agreements as delivering more advantages to the big business at the expense of workers.

With the election of Trump as the US President, the future course of the TPP was thrown into chaos. For Trump, the main target of his trade policy is to contain China. He did not mince words in accusing China as an "unfair" trading country. His accusation list was long: currency manipulation, stealing intellectual property right, mandatory technology transfer, denial of market access for American firms, limiting competition, monopoly power of state-owned enterprise, dumping and illegal subsidy, and so on. In his plan for reforming US trade relations with China, he stated that he

---

41 Requoted from Barfield (2016)

42 Requoted from Barfield (2016)

would formally designate China a currency manipulator, crack down on its theft of US intellectual property, and expose its various export subsidy practices.

With the benefit of hindsight, Obama should have moved faster. Concluding the TPP in October 2016, just a year away from the US Presidential election was not earning sufficient time for clearing a path toward ratification. It should be noted that the US negotiators did not have the TPA until the mid-2015. Without TPA, the US Congress could amend the outcome of the TPP as agreed between the US administration and 11 other countries. Hence, the other 11 countries were persistently demanding the US to get the TPA. They were aware of the disastrous possibility of no implementation of a hard-won agreement, in case of negotiations without TPA. It was May 2015 when the Obama administration got the TPA.

Expected Effect of the TPP[43]

There are three layers in the TPP: agreement related to the old economy; so-called Singapore Issues (investment, competition, procurement, trade facilitation); and agreement related to the new economy, mainly digital trade and GVC.

As for the grand strategy in the era of the steady decline of US power coupled with the rise of China in the global stage, the TPP is a "rebalancing

---

43 This section draws on Choi (2016).

to Asia" in order to contain China. In an affirmative sense, the TPP was the US grand strategy to lead the way in the 21st century. By creating a critical mass on the new trade rule with high standards, the TPP was expected to induce participating countries to reform themselves pursuant to the principle of competitive liberal market economy.

The TPP would not stop with the 12 initial signatories. The TPP was designed to serve as a platform for expanding membership. Expectation was high that TPP will become a de facto standard for future trade agreements. Several countries, which stood outside the TPP talks, may try to accede to the TPP. It could create a tipping point that more and more countries would want to join the TPP, while RCEP would lose momentum. Through this process, China may be isolated.

With the US withdrawal from the TPP in 2017 by Trump, paradoxically, the RCEP seems like it is also losing momentum. ASEAN, the backbone of the membership formation of the RCEP, has been failing to lead the talks. China's desire to exert its influence in the Asian trade architecture has not translated into its leadership. In spite of long talks on the virtue of free and open trade, as in Xi's speech in Davos 2017, China does not have the political will to open up further, especially their service sectors, including financial services.

5. Emergence of TPP 11 without the US

President Trump pulled the US out of the TPP in his first week in office.

His campaign pledge had become a harsh reality to the other 11 TPP signatories. The largest stakeholder of the TPP turned its back on the very project it promoted as the 21st century global trade architecture. Trump's action would be recorded in history as a defining moment of "Globalization without America."[44]

The biggest disappointment was coming from Japan. Prime Minister Abe played TPP as an integral part of his revitalization program of Japan and strategy to confront the rise of assertive China. Abe threw his political asset to salvage the TPP before President Trump officially acted to withdraw the US from the TPP. Immediately after the election of Trump, Abe flew to the US and met with Trump in his dire effort to persuade the newly-elected US President of the significance of the TPP.

Responding to Trump's decision to withdraw, Abe said it was "meaningless" to pursue TPP without the world's largest economy. Many commentators shared the same view. They thought that the TPP would sink and disappear from the public eye. Tokyo's calculations, however, would soon change. Once it became clear to Abe that all those desperate efforts were of no avail, he worked to salvage "TPP without America." Plan B was to have the TPP intact among the other 11 signatories. Japan and some like-minded middle powers, including Australia, worked to save the TPP.

Many countries in the TPP had a bilateral FTA with the US. Notable

---

44 "US withdrawal from the TPP is grand gift to China" Financial Times, 2017.

absence is Japan, Malaysia, and Vietnam. As for Vietnam, the TPP meant Factory Vietnam. Political elites of Vietnam intended to emulate the success of Factory China by securing preferential access to the US, while China would be denied of the same privilege. Political leaders of Vietnam took the TPP as unmistakable opportunity for the country to emerge as a GVC. In order to get closer to their strategic vision, Vietnam swallowed hard and accepted the rules of the 21st Century, and rules on SOE, Competition, Environment, and Labor despite domestic opposition. With the departure of the US from the TPP, salvaging the TPP with the other 11 countries would not mean that much to Vietnam. For similar reasons, some countries were suspicious of the benefits of rescuing the TPP without America. Notwithstanding, negotiating efforts and political will of the remaining 11 countries proved such conjecture wrong.

In the margin of the APEC Leaders Meeting in Da Nang, Vietnam, November 2017, the 11 TPP signatories convened and agreed to rescue the TPP in the name of Comprehensive and Progressive Agreement for TPP (CPTPP). (In this book, "TPP 11" and "CPTPP" are used to mean the same agreement). After a couple of months, any remaining differences were ironed out. After a year from the very same day of the US withdrawal from the TPP (January 23, 2018), the remaining 11 signatories of the TPP announced that they agreed on the CPTPP.

The agreement remains substantially the same as the TPP, but contains a list of 20 "suspended provisions" that were added to the TPP at the U.S.'s insistence and that are now no longer binding. These provisions primarily relate to investment, government procurement, and intellectual property. In March 2018, CPTPP was signed by those 11 countries. After the CPTPP comes into force, it would be open to other non-signatory economies. Korea, Indonesia, Thailand, the Philippines, and Taiwan have expressed interest in taking part. Recently, the UK also indicated its interest.

What drove the remaining 11 signatories to rescue the TPP without the US? Three factors were at play. **First, economic effect.** The remaining 11 countries came to realize the benefit from reduced trade barriers even without the US.[45] **Second, preemptive rule setting.** As discussed before, the TPP had several rules on the New Economy, including E-Commerce, and on the issues outside of the WTO system (SOE, Competition, IPR, Government Procurement, and so on). Setting trade rules on these issues would provide significant negotiating leverage in future contest of trade architecture. The on-going RCEP negotiates those agenda but the bars are set low. Strong rules on those agenda at the TPP 11 would preempt negotiations on other fora. In particular, those rules would be pressed on the assertive China to enhance its commitment to those key issues. **Third, strategic factor.** Japan is still hopeful that the US would return to the TPP eventually. To induce the US, Tokyo thinks, having the TPP up and running may be a more effective strategy than having no TPP at all. Upsurge of

45 Shujiro Urata from Waseda University economist forecast a boost of 0.9 per cent to the Japanese economy once the CPTPP is enforced. He argued this was "not a small number" for Japan, growing about one per cent a year on average. (Sim 2018)

Australian beef and increased sale of Chilean wine in Japan would prompt disgruntled American farmers to blame the absence of the US in the TPP 11. Their angry voices may tilt the political equilibrium. Those were strategic calculation on the mindset of the TPP 11 rescuers.[46]

Whether they really believe that way is unclear. Such wishful thinking is driving the current trade Japanese strategy in the era of the TPP without the US. Against the rising tide of protectionism, the TPP 11 is regarded as firm commitment to free and open trade. In particular, the TPP 11 means a lot to Japan. Japan has never played a main role in initiating significant plurilateral trade agreement. Even at the peak of its economic power, Japan's power was unidimensional. Economic power was not translated into soft power or political power. Japan was content in the position of being second behind the initiative of the US.

In the postwar global affairs, there has been no single multilateral initiative in which Japan championed. Japan developed a pattern of following the cue of the US. And it became an addictive habit. This time was different. Japan hesitated a bit after the US disappeared from the stage. History was against the side of Japan. Economic stakes became smaller. Pessimistic sentiment ran high. Once it realized multi-faceted significance

46 At international conference hosted by the TCS in Seoul 2017, a panelist from Japan in the session where I moderated claimed that the US would eventually return to the TPP. He was drawing on historical episode where the US created the GATT in 1947, after it failed to ratify the International Trade Organization before.

of TPP without America, Japan championed the case for TPP 11 and went all the way to the conclusion of it. Japan threw political weight in salvaging the TPP. It built a strong case for the TPP 11 in saving free and open economy from the headwind of protectionism.

After years of negotiations since 2013, RCEP talks are yet to be done. The 16 participating countries have missed self-declared deadline after deadline. ASEAN wants to exercise the principle of ASEAN Centrality but without political clout. Japan and Australia would not be willing to accept any concessions lower than those secured in TPP 11. Under this complicated situation, can China exercise political leadership?

China pushed the RCEP as alternative to the TPP. Two factors may stand in the way of advancing the RCEP to conclusion. First, some members may not be cooperative to China's drive. Japan in particular would find no compelling reason to follow the lead of China. In order to induce Japan to the conclusion of the RCEP, China should be able to offer attractive terms for Japan's access to the Chinese market. Considering the Chinese negotiating strategy, it would be a tall order. Second, China might have lost the sense of urgency, after Trump pulled the US out of the TPP. More importantly, the RCEP may be a half-way house even in the case of successful agreement, due to its less-comprehensive coverage of the agenda and lack of liberalization. Hence, the TPP 11, rather than the RCEP, holds a strong chance for being promoted as a model for future mega FTAs.

6. Intensifying Competition for Strategic Preemption in Northeast Asia

In parallel with the trade architecture competition, policy makers in Seoul, Tokyo, and Beijing allocated substantial amount of resources in pushing forward its bilateral trade networks with major trading partners. Three major developments were seen: The Korea-China FTA, the Japan-EU FTA, and China's BIT talks with the US and with the EU. At last, Seoul responded to many years of request from Beijing to negotiate the Korea-China FTA. Seoul and Beijing came to agree on the Korea-China FTA in the late 2014. A year later, it came into force. Korea had become the one and only Asian nation who has preferential access to the US, the EU, and China through an FTA. In parallel with these developments, Korea, Japan, and China finally came to an agreement on their trilateral investment treaty.

China-Japan-Korea Investment Agreement

China has become the largest host country for FDI in the developing world and a major investment destination for Japan and Korea, whose outward FDI stock in China in 2012 was $93 billion and $51 billion, respectively. Nearly three-fourths of Japanese and Korean foreign investment goes to China's manufacturing sector. By contrast, Chinese FDI stock in Japan and Korea remains limited to just $500 million and $3 billion, respectively, which amounts to 0.3 and 2.1 percent of total Chinese investment abroad. Similarly, Korean investment in Japan is limited, around $4 billion in 2012, which is 2 percent of total Korean investment abroad. These imbalances gave the impetus for concluding an investment agreement that would not only expand investment opportunities in China but also promote Chinese participation in the underinvested (in relative terms) Korean and Japanese markets.

Compared to other high-level investment agreements, China-Japan-Korea Investment Agreement is assessed to be rather weak in the protection of investors and in the investment liberalization.[47] When it comes to investment protection, the protection offered to foreign investors under the CJK treaty is assessed to be insufficient, inadequate, sometimes opaque, therefore, subject to regulatory risks of the host country. Interestingly, the trilateral CJK investment treaty offers less investment liberalization than the bilateral Korea-Japan investment treaty does. (Table 9) In terms of national treatment, performance requirement, and transfer of fund, CJK is assessed to be less strong than Korea-Japan BIT.

47 Schott and Cimino (2015) in comparison to the Investment Chapter of the KORUS and the TPP.

Figure 6. Investment Agreements in Northeast Asia

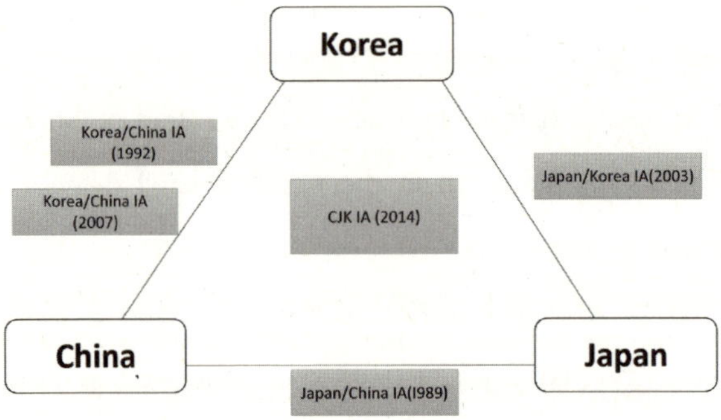

Bilateral Investment Agreement (IA) (also called as BIT: Bilateral Investment Treaty) were signed and in effect between Korea-Japan, Korea-China, and China-Japan. Korea-China IA of 1992 was replaced by new Korea-China IA of 2007. Trilateral investment agreement among Korea, Japan, and China were signed on May 2012, and went into effect as of May 2014.

Number indicates the year when the agreement went into force.

Table 9. CJK Investment Agreement vs Korea-Japan BIT

		CJK Investment Treaty(2014)	Korea-Japan BIT(2003)
National Treatment	Pre-investment	No	Yes
	Post-investment	standstill	Yes
MFN	Pre-investment	Yes	Yes
	Post-investment	Yes	Yes
Performance Requirement	Export restriction	Yes	No
	Local materials	Yes	Yes
	Local content	Yes	Yes
	Ex-im balancing	Yes	Yes
	Export requirement	unreasonable & discriminatory	Yes
	Local sales restriction	No	yes

	Nationality of executives	No	yes
	Local employment	No	yes
	Headquarter location requirement	No	yes
	R&D requirement	No	yes
	Technology transfer	unreasonable & discriminatory	yes
	Exclusive supply	No	yes
Negative list		No	yes
Transfer of funds		approval within 2 months	yes

**Source: Nakagawa (2014)

Korea-China FTA[48]

As Korea's largest trade and investment partner, China was a logical FTA partner for Korea. However, it took a long time for Korea and China to come to the negotiation table for their bilateral FTA. As discussed before, China as a Socialist regime with a closer link to North Korea than South Korea presented a different level of challenges to the Korean policy makers. Preparation for negotiations consumed considerable time. The Korean and Chinese governments' joint study for the feasibility of the Korea-China FTA dates back to September 2005. Bilateral negotiations started seven years later in May 2012, during the final year of President Lee Myung-bak's administration. In November 2014, Korea and China announced that they

48 Discussion in this section draws on Chi and Oh (2017)

reached an agreement.

The outcome fell short of a high-level FTA. Both sides played a defensive game. The Korean side was defensive due to strong protectionist demand from small and medium-sized industries in manufacturing sectors (e.g., light industries) that faced competition from low-priced Chinese imports. Moreover, the agricultural sector was strongly against further liberalization to China.

Unlike Korea's negotiations with the US and the EU, Korea was not eager to make major concessions on market access to enhance its market access to the other country.

In addition, political leadership created a negotiating environment that was unfavorable to secure a comprehensive FTA. President Park Geun-hye's administration was anxious to expeditiously conclude its FTA negotiations with China for political reasons. During a series of summit meetings in 2014, President Park Geun-hye and President Xi Jinping agreed, confirmed, and renewed their pledge to conclude the Korea-China FTA talks within 2014. Strong political pressure from the leadership to the negotiators worked against the free trade group and more favorably for the protectionist group. Under time pressure, negotiators had enormous difficulties overcoming the protectionist bias at the negotiating table.

Ultimately, the Korea-China FTA resulted in less market opening compared to Korea's FTAs with other major trade partners, such as the United States and the EU. Under the Korea-China FTA, 10 percent of products in terms of tariff line and 15 percent of products in terms of trade volume were excluded from negotiations for tariff elimination, whereas all products except rice were subject to tariff elimination negotiations under the Korea-US FTA and the Korea-EU FTA. Moreover, the Korean government did not make significant agricultural concessions in the Korea-China FTA.

The liberalization ratio (the coverage of product subject to preferential tariff cut) of the Korean agricultural sector is 70 percent in terms of tariff line and 40 percent in terms of import volume in the Korea-China FTA, compared to 98.3 percent and 92.5 percent, respectively, in the Korea-US FTA. In prior FTAs with the United States and the EU, the Korean government had agreed to eventual tariff elimination for all agricultural products except for rice. In contrast, most agricultural products, including rice, pepper, garlic, onions, apples, pears, grapes, oranges, beef, pork, chicken, duck, potatoes, cheese, honey, and milk, were excluded from tariff concessions in the Korea-China FTA. As a result, Chinese farmers will continue to face higher tariffs compared to their US and European counterparts. Korea's smaller agricultural concessions came at the cost of smaller Chinese tariff concessions on industrial products. China agreed to eliminate tariffs for 71.7 percent of product line and 66.4 percent of import volume by the tenth year after the Korea-China FTA goes into effect.

The Korean government failed to secure preferential market access to China in several product lines of steel, petrochemical, automobiles, and automobile parts. Domestic response to the Korea-China FTA outcome was less sanguine on the grounds that it failed to create more jobs in Korea's competitive sectors in order to protect its uncompetitive agricultural sector. Of all the FTAs concluded by Korea, the Korea-China FTA may be the largest in trade terms, but is assessed to be far from the best in terms of the depth of liberalization and the scope of obligation.

Tokyo's Game Plan

Tokyo launched FTA negotiations with Brussels, at the same time when it decided to join the TPP talks. It was a simultaneous move by Tokyo. The move intended to address trade diversion effect caused by the Korea-EU FTA. Such a Japanese strategic move resembled a Korean move several years earlier: Seoul launched FTA negotiations with Brussels immediately after it started FTA talks with the US. What had worked for Korea was also working for Japan: visionary leadership and cohesive domestic trade governance. In December 2017, the two heads of states from Japan and the EU announced that they reached an agreement. The Japan-EU EPA, the official name of the FTA between Japan and the EU, is expected to be effective from 2018 at the earliest. Technically speaking, they do not have the complete text for domestic approval. Japan and the EU have not yet resolved their different stances on the issue of investment protection. In order to expedite the process of domestic approval, the two sides agreed to move on to the next stage, while they continue to negotiate on investment protection.

One needs to note that Japan made a great deal of concession in the agriculture sector. With regards to agricultural exports from the EU, the agreement will scrap duties on many cheeses such as Gouda and Cheddar (which currently are at 29.8%) as well as on wine exports (currently at 15% on average); allow the EU to increase its beef exports to Japan substantially, while on pork there will be duty-free trade in processed meat and near-duty-free trade for fresh meat; ensure protection of more than 200 high-quality European agricultural products in Japan, so-called Geographical Indications (GIs), and will also ensure protection of a selection of Japanese GIs in the EU.[49]

Japan's commitment in its FTA with the EU is something equivalent to its commitment in the TPP. With the successful conclusion of TPP and the completion of the Japan-EU FTA, at last Japan got even with Korea in terms of preferential access to the US and the EU. Because of the departure of the US from the TPP, Japan's strategy did not fully work out. Nonetheless, Japan's entry into TPP talks was a game-changing move for Japan's trade policy and competition for future trade architecture.

Beijing's Game Plan

While Japan was making strides in advancing its bilateral FTA networks with major trading partners, China was also making its move on those major players. Because of negotiating approaches of the US and the EU, which sought for comprehensive and in-depth liberalization in goods, services, and

49 EU homepage.

investment, China planned a two-stage approach: first, negotiate a BIT, and afterwards, negotiate an FTA, if the time is appropriate. The two-step gradual approach fully manifested constraints and dilemma Beijing was facing.

At the present, China's two-step approach has not delivered any tangible outcome. China's BIT talks with the US date back to 2008. The pace of negotiation was uneven and non-linear. The US requested China to come up with a negative list of investment liberalization, which would list sectors where foreign investment will be restricted (all other sectors will be open). It took years for Beijing to prepare the draft version of the negative list to advance the negotiations. The initial negative list was reportedly quite long, and fell short of US expectation. The US demand for a revision, which was met with the Chinese resistance. So far, more than two dozen rounds of negotiations were held. China's negative list was revised a couple of times. The BIT talks were intensified during the later years of President Obama, but still fell short of reaching an agreement.

The U.S. aimed for an enforceable, high-standard, and comprehensive BIT with China. Such a BIT would provide opportunities to expand market access for U.S. firms and address growing concerns about Chinese policies that disadvantage US investment, in particular favorable treatment of Chinese domestic firms at the expense of foreign firms (including subsidization of domestic competitors, foreign investment restrictions, unequal and sometimes targeted law enforcement and implementation, weak enforcement of IPR, and lack of transparency).[50]

To Beijing, the bad news is that the Trump administration does not attach high priority on the BIT talks with China. The good news is that the US has not shut the door on the BIT. US top trade officials indicated that there were still some issues to be cleared up before moving on to BIT. Perhaps the US-China BIT might be given a chance to be concluded before Trump's term is over.

China's negotiations with the EU on BIT started later than its BIT negotiations with the US. With the delay of the US-China BIT talks, and with the ever-mounting pressure of the US-led mega FTA initiative of TPP and TTIP (Trans-Atlantic Trade and Investment Partnership), China turned to the EU to launch FTA negotiations. China was absent from both the Trans-Pacific (TPP) and the Trans-Atlantic (TTIP) trade initiatives. China was fearful of a negative trade diversion effect. China was also afraid of having to follow new "global" standards set by others. As for the European side, it wanted greater openings into China and a level-playing field with domestic companies. In March 2014, Brussels agreed that once an EU-China investment treaty is concluded, it will consider broader trade talks with Beijing. The investment treaty negotiations had begun just a few months

50 According to the USTR (2012), a high-standard BIT based on the U.S. model provides investors with "improved market access; protection from discriminatory, expropriatory, or otherwise harmful government treatment; and a mechanism to pursue binding international arbitration for breaches of the treaty"; in addition, a high-standard BIT "improves investment climates, promotes market-based economic reform, and strengthens the rule of law." (USTR 2012)

before, in November 2013. In case of successful conclusion of the China-EU BIT, this BIT would replace the 26 existing BITs that China has signed over the years with individual EU member states. Having the BIT between Beijing and Brussels would open a door for FTA negotiations between them. At the present, the BIT still remains at the negotiating table.

So far, Beijing's two-step approach with the US and the EU has not produced any outcome, even in the first step. While those negotiations were unfolding, Beijing was going through a high-stake internal contest between reformers and nationalists. Due to China's steady rise in economic development in the early part of the new millennium, China's status has elevated to the largest middle-income country with a striking distance of overtaking the US in terms of total GDP. Besides the accusation of currency manipulation, policy makers in Beijing knew to their heart that they could not continue the conventional modus operandi of growth strategy. Beijing came up with a transition plan to transform from a high growth model to a high quality model. Under the plan, China would move up the value chain and shift from a low-end manufacturing economy to a higher-end technology and knowledge economy. Such a transition would require recalibration of domestic investment away from hard infrastructure to soft innovation. Consumer consumption needs to be increased. These recognitions drove China to come up with the Decision on Deepening of Reforms at the 18th Central Committee Third Plenary Session 2013. The question is: *Will China implement these reform plans?*

7. Domestic Trade Governance Structure

While Korea's advance in creating trade preemption was ahead of the game in Northeast Asia during the first decade of the new millennium, Japan's efforts to get even with Korea was remarkable in the second decade. Korea's FTA talks with the US were the game changing move for Korea. Japan's game changing move was to join the TPP talks, which were under the leadership of the US. Through this strategic competition, both Korea and Japan have distanced themselves from China. Thanks to their trade negotiations with the US, Korea and Japan achieved a high-level FTA, which in turn prompted them to pursue a similar level of FTAs with other advanced countries.

Korea's trade (imports and exports) with the 52 countries with which it has signed FTAs (there are 15 agreements altogether) amounted to US$350.4 billion in the first half of the year, which accounted for 68.2% of the country's total trade (US$513.5 billion) over that period. Korea's FTA partners accounted for 83.5 percent of Korea's food import, while Japan's FTA partners accounted for 39.9 percent of Japan's food import.[51] If the TPP 11 and the EU are to be included, the number for Japan would substantially increase, even though it would still fall short on the number for Korea.

Considering Korea's head start in moving toward high-level FTA, it is

51 Choi and Oh (2017).

quite puzzling to see Korea's absence in the TPP talks. A remarkable development since 2013 is that Korea seems trapped in a bilateral mode, while Japan became more flexible in the venue of trade liberalization. What has caused this asymmetry? Trade governance and political leadership are critical factors.[52]

Since 2013, Korea's hitherto cohesive domestic trade governance has transformed into a less cohesive one. The new government of Korea replaced MOFAT (Ministry of Foreign Affairs and Trade) with MOTIE (Ministry of Trade, Industry and Energy). In the process, greater sectoral interests surged to the fore in the trade policy coordination process. Unlike MOFAT, under which there were no sectoral representations, MOTIE proved vulnerable to protectionist demands. In particular, the main constituents of MOTIE, such as the heavy and chemical industries and SMEs, demanded their sectoral concerns ahead of greater national interest. As a result, even though MOTIE still carried the full negotiating authority for FTA policies, it was less inclined to pursue ambitious FTAs at the expense of liberalizing import-competing industries.

In contrast, Japan's domestic trade governance is increasingly becoming more cohesive under the leadership of Abe. Specifically, the creation of the TPP taskforce in 2013 has centralized the authority and decision-making process for trade policies, replacing its prior decentralized system where

52 The following analysis draws on Choi and Oh (2017).

independent ministries negotiated separately on trade policy items. The strategic weakening of Japan's powerful farm group by Abe played a pivotal role. These changes have enabled national interests, rather than narrow sectoral interests, to play a greater role in Japan's trade policy-making process.

With time-lag, what has worked wonders for Korea also worked for Japan. Japan could not pursue an FTA with the United States, despite possible trade diversion effects arising from KORUS. Its fragmented trade governance stood in the way. With changes to a more cohesive coordination mechanism under strong political leadership, Japan could overcome the agricultural liberalization taboo and take part in the TPP negotiations as well as pursue FTAs with major agricultural exporting countries.

Had Korea's domestic trade governance been more cohesive, Korea could have pursued the TPP negotiations. Post-2013 domestic trade governance regimes in Japan and Korea are still unfolding. The continuation and durability of the institutional changes that have occurred in Japan's and Korea's domestic trade governance have important consequences for the future.

Table 10. Share of Food Import in Japan's FTA

	Partner	Status	Share of Japan's Food Imports in 2013
Japan	Singapore	Effectuated 11/2002	0.9%
	Mexico	Effectuated 04/2005	1.4%
	Malaysia	Effectuated 07/2006	0.6%
	Chile	Effectuated 09/2007	2.7%
	Thailand	Effectuated 11/2007	6.1%
	Indonesia	Effectuated 07/2008	1.7%
	Brunei	Effectuated 07/2008	0.0%
	ASEAN	Effectuated 12/2008	13.2%*
	Philippines	Effectuated 12/2008	1.9%
	Switzerland	Effectuated 09/2009	1.0%
	Vietnam	Effectuated 10/2009	1.9%
	India	Effectuated 08/2011	1.4%
	Peru	Effectuated 03/2012	0.30%
	Australia	Effectuated 01/2015	6.20%
	Mongolia	Effectuated 06/2016	NA
		Total	**39.9 %**

Japan concluded CPTPP with ten countries. In the table above, CPTPP is not covered, because it is yet to be effective.

**Source: Japan Statistical Yearbook (2015). Choi and Oh (2017)

Table 11. Share of Food Import in Koreas FTA

	Partner	Status	Share of Korea's Food Imports in 2015
Korea	Chile	Effectuated 04/2004	2.92%
	Singapore	Effectuated 03/2006	0.45%
	EFTA	Effectuated 09/2006	0.29%
	ASEAN	Effectuated 06/2007	13.21%
	India	Effectuated 01/2010	3.37%
	EU	Effectuated 07/2011	10.62%
	Peru	Effectuated 08/2011	0.19%
	US	Effectuated 03/2012	19.61%
	Turkey	Effectuated 05/2013	0.21%
	Australia	Effectuated 12/2014	7.7%
	Canada	Effectuated 01/2015	4.42%
	China	Effectuated 12/2015	15.55%
	New Zealand	Effectuated 12/2015	3.11%
	Vietnam	Effectuated 12/2015	1.96%
	Columbia	Effectuated 07/2016	0.24%
		Total	**83.5 %**

**Source: Choi and Oh (2017)

8. Appraisal and Summary

General picture and major features of trade performance in Northeast Asia in the second decade of the 21st century is summarized as follows:

1. Overall, trade among Northeast Asia has been on the rise. Compared to the beginning of the 21st century, China's trade to Japan and Korea has increased by four times, likewise for Korea's trade to Japan and China. Japan's trade to Korea and China has increased by three times.

2. Compared to the first decade, trade performance in Northeast Asia countries in the second decade. Shows interesting contrast. In the first decade all bilateral trade among Northeast Asia have increased. In the second decade both trade between Japan and China and trade between Korea and Japan have become stagnant. In particular, Japan's export to China and Kore's export to Japan has declined. Notably, trade between Korea and China has increased. China has become Korea's number 1 exporting destination with its quarter of Korea's export to China. As for China, the US has been the largest trade partner for its export with 18% of export share. As for Japan, both the US and China have been two largest trade partners for its exports. Relative significance of the US market for export destination is lowest in Korea (13%), compared to the US share in China (18%) and Japan (20%). (Table 12. 13. 14)

After spending the first decade of the 21st century in negotiating bilateral FTA, Korea, Japan and China moved on to regional and mega-regional FTA in the second decade. If bilateral FTA is something like connecting dots to create lines, regional and mega-regional FTA is to connect lines to create space. What has occurred in the second decade of the 21st in the Northeast Asia trade architecture competition is summarized and assessed as follows:

1. The driving force of trade architecture competition was the TPP. The US defined the TPP as the rule-setting for the 21st century trade. Japan joined the TPP. Japan's transformation of its domestic trade governance from fragmented to cohesive enabled Japan's participation in the TPP.

2. Korea, which was most active in pursuing high-level FTA in the first

decade, was reluctant to join the TPP, and decided to remain outside of the TPP talks. Instead Korea negotiated bilateral FTA with China, which is regarded as low-level with a substantial scope and coverage for exception from tariff elimination and no commitment on services. Korea's decision and choice reflected its domestic trade governance change to fragmented structure from cohesive one.

3. In order to counter the TPP driven by the US, China resorted to launch the RCEP and the BRI. The negotiating agenda of the RCEP is less comprehensive than that of the TPP. The level of ambition of the RCEP in achieving trade liberalization is lower than that of the TPP.

4. Even though the TPP came to the conclusion, it failed to become effective. The largest stakeholder of the TPP, the US, withdrew from the TPP, stopping its ratification process. Remarkably, the US withdrawal from the TPP did not lead to the total collapse of the TPP. Japan worked with other remaining countries in the TPP and resurrected the TPP in the form of the CPTPP. The CPTPP is in effect the TPP without the US. Establishing the CPTPP is a silver lining in the midst of stormy clouds of protectionism.

5. Korea, Japan, and China are in the negotiations for CJK and for RCEP. Japan is in the CPTPP, while both Korea and China have not joined. CJK FTA talks have been launched after a long period of preparation. So far, the progress has been slow and negotiations are still at an early stage.

6. Trilateral negotiations among Korea, Japan and China to create deeper trade architecture have led to the CJK Investment Treaty. In terms of investment liberalization and investment protection, the CJK Investment

Treaty is evaluated to be weak, due to China's lack of open and reform in investment. Korea and Japan strongly want to upgrade CJK Investment Treaty.

7. There is a strong correlation between dominant ideology of a nation and its performance of FTA. When globalism is dominant ideology in a nation, the nation is more likely to pursue high-level FTA. When nationalism is dominant ideology in a nation, the nation tends to pursue low-level FTA. When globalism was more dominant than nationalism, Korea produced high-level FTA, as seen in the case of KORUS and the Korea-US FTA, and Japan negotiated high-level FTA such as TPP, CPTPP, and Japan-EU FTA. In case of China, nationalism has been dominant than globalism, leading to China's low-level FTAs so far. (Table 19)

Table 12. China's export statistics (US $ million)

	2016		2010		2008		2001	
US	385,678	*18*	283,780	*18*	252,844	*18*	54,355	*20*
ASEAN	224,508	*11*	122,937	*8*	109,217	*8*	NA	-
Japan	129,268	*6*	121,044	*8*	116,132	*8*	44,941	*17*
Korea	93,707	*4*	68,047	*4*	73,932	*5*	12,519	*5*
Germany	65,214	*3*	68,047	*4*	59,209	*4*	9,751	*4*
UK	55,664	*3*	38,767	*2*	36,073	*3*	6,781	*3*
France	24,959	*1*	27,859	*2*	23,499	*2*	3,701	*1*
Total	2,097,637		1577,764		1,430,693		266,098	

Italic shows trade share of exporting destination out of China's total export
NA = non-available

**Source: World Bank, ASEAN

Table 13. Korea's export statistics (unit: $1,000,000) (US $ million)

	2016		2010		2008		2001	
China	124,433	*25*	116,838	*25*	91,388	*22*	18,186	*12*
ASEAN	78,540	*16*	56,965	*12*	41,804	*10*	NA	-
US	66,748	*13*	49,991	*11*	46,500	*11*	31,357	*21*
Japan	24,354	*5*	28,176	*6*	28,252	*7*	16,502	*11*
UK	6,922	*1*	5,555	*1*	5,936	*1*	3,490	*2*
Germany	6,443	*1*	10,702	*2*	10,522	*2*	4,322	*3*
France	2,504	*1*	3,042	*1*	3,683	*1*	1,599	*1*
Total	495,418		466,381		422,003		150,431	

Italic shows trade share of exporting destination out of Korea's total export
NA = non-available

**Source: World Bank, ASEAN

Table 14. Japan's export statistics (US $ million)

	2016		2010		2008		2001	
US	130,586	*20*	120,338	*16*	138,705	*18*	122,543	*30*
China	113,830	*18*	149,451	*19*	124,901	*16*	30,994	*8*
ASEAN	105,856	*16*	115,936	*15*	108,897	*14*	NA	-
Korea	46,235	*7*	62,361	*8*	59,493	*8*	25,297	*6*
Germany	17,653	*3*	20,290	*3*	23,955	*3*	15,620	*4*
UK	13,659	*2*	14,174	*2*	16,464	*2*	12,147	*3*
France	6,240	*1*	6,706	*1*	9,112	*1*	6,281	*2*
Total	644,932		769,774		781,412		403,344	

Italic shows trade share of exporting destination out of Japan's total export
NA = non-available

**Source: World Bank, ASEAN

Table 15. China's import statistics (US $ million)

	2016		2010		2008		2001	
US	135,120	*8.6*	102,734	*7.4*	81,585	*7.2*	26,217	*10.8*
ASEAN	14,846	*1*	22,963	*1.7*	21.468	*1.9*	2,312	*1*
Japan	145,670	*9.2*	176,736	*12.7*	150,600	*13.3*	42,787	*17.6*
Korea	158,974	*10*	138,339	*9.9*	112,137	*9.9*	23,376	*9.6*
Germany	86,109	*5.4*	74,251	*5.3*	55,789	*4.9*	13,772	*5.7*
UK	18,681	*1.2*	11,305	*0.8*	9.541	*0.8*	3,526	*1.5*
France	22,511	*1.4*	17,116	*1,2*	15,644	*1.4*	4,106	*1.7*
Total	1,587,920		1,396,001		1,132,562		243,552	

Italic shows trade share of importing destination out of China's total import

**Source: World Bank

Table 16. Korea's import statistics (US $ million)

	2016		2010		2008		2001	
US	43,397	*10.7*	40,588	*9.6*	38,555	*8.7*	22,430	*15.9*
ASEAN	4,856	*1.2*	6,272	*1.5*	7,442	*1.7*	1,496	*1.1*
Japan	47,466	*11.7*	64,295	*15.1*	60,956	*14*	26,633	*18.9*
China	86,978	*21.4*	71,573	*16.8*	76,926	*17.7*	13,302	*9.4*
Germany	18,916	*4.7*	14,304	*3.4*	14,769	*3.4*	4,473	*3.2*
UK	5,211	*1.3*	3,265	*0.8*	3,637	*0.8*	2,353	*1.7*
France	5,847	*1.4*	4,289	*1*	4,885	*1.1*	2,096	*1.5*
Total	406,181		425,208		435,271		141,097	

Italic shows trade share of importing destination out of Korea's total import

**Source: World Bank

Table 17. Japan's import statistics (unit: $1,000,000) (US $ million)

	2016		2010		2008		2001	
US	69,221	*11.4*	69,114	*10*	78,937	*10.4*	63,756	*18.3*
ASEAN	6,414	*1.1*	6,660	*1*	6,118	*0.8*	2,775	*0.8*
China	156,552	*25.8*	153,203	*22.1*	143,229	*18.8*	57,864	*16.6*
Korea	25,019	*4.1*	28,600	*4.1*	29,475	*3.9*	17,197	*4.5*
Germany	22,022	*3.7*	19,291	*2.8*	20,852	*2.7*	12,400	*3.6*
UK	6,511	*1.1*	6,387	*0.9*	7,473	*1*	6,003	*1.7*
France	10,218	*1.7*	10,300	*1.5*	10,642	*1.4*	6,182	*1.8*
Total	606,924		694,059		762,533		349,291	

Italic shows trade share of importing destination out of Japan's total import

**Source: World Bank

Figure 7. Variable Geometry of FTA involving Northeast Asian countries

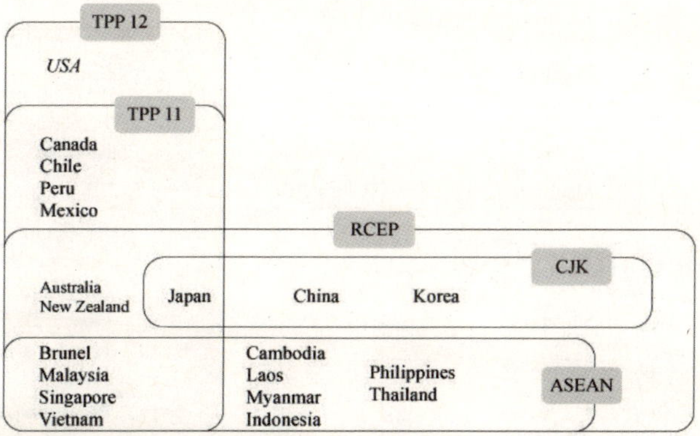

Countries in Northeast Asia have been negotiating for various regional FTAs.
Korea, Japan, and China are in the negotiations for CJK and for RCEP.
Japan is in the TPP 11, formally known as CPTPP, while both Korea and China have not joined.

Table 18. FTA partners of China, Japan, and South Korea (as of Jan 2018)

	China	Japan	South Korea
Concluded	Hong Kong, China	Singapore	Chile
	Macao, China	Mexico	Singapore
	ASEAN	Malaysia	European Free Trade Association
	Chile	Chile	ASEAN
	Pakistan	Thailand	India
	New Zealand	ASEAN	EU
	Singapore	Brunei Darussalam	Peru
	Peru	Indonesia	The United States
	Costa Rica	Philippines	Turkey
	Iceland	Switzerland	Colombia
	Switzerland	Vietnam	Australia
	Korea	India	Canada
	Australia	Peru	China
	Georgia	Australia	New Zealand
	Maldives	Mongolia	Vietnam
		TPP	
Under negotiation	Moldova	Columbia	China-Japan
	Mauritius	China-Korea	RCEP
	Singapore	EU	6 countries in Central America (Panama, Costa Rica, Guatemala, Honduras, El Salvador, Nicaragua)
	Norway	Turkey	Ecuador
	Israel	RCEP	Israel
	Sri Lanka	Gulf Cooperation Council	
	Japan-Korea	Korea	
	Gulf Cooperation Council	Canada	
	RCEP		

Table19. Relationship between Ideology and FTA in Northeast Asia

Dominant Ideology / Characteristics of FTAs	Globalism	Nationalism
High level FTA (comprehensive liberalization)	Korea (1998-2012) Japan (post-2013)	
Low level FTA (protectionist)		Japan (1990-2012) Korea (post-2013) China

There is a strong correlation between dominant ideology of a nation and its performance of FTA.

When globalism is dominant ideology in a nation, the nation is more likely to pursue high-level FTA.

When nationalism is dominant ideology in a nation, the nation tends to pursue low-level FTA.

When globalism was more dominant than nationalism, Korea produced high-level FTA, as seen in the case of KORUS and the Korea-US FTA, and Japan negotiated high-level FTA such as TPP, CPTPP, and Japan-EU FTA. In case of China, nationalism has been dominant than globalism, leading to China's low-level FTAs so far.

**Source: Author's illustration

5 Emergence of the New Normal

1. Beginning of the End

No single event would better illustrate the beginning of the end of the normal (the existing international economic order) than the failure to secure ratification of the TPP in the US. Closer scrutiny of the unravelling of the TPP unveils underlying currents and dynamism which would surface soon.

To give a quick review of the situation, the TPP was signed by 12 negotiating countries in early 2016. To be effective, TPP should be ratified in the US. Otherwise, TPP would remain a lame document on the desk.[53] As it turns out, the year 2016 was a time for the election of the U.S. President and Congress. The Obama administration, which promoted the TPP as a trade rule for the 21st century, seriously sought its ratification at Congress, but in vain. Some said the time for ratification was not sufficient. The window

53 This is due to the TPP agreement on the entry into force. Even if all other 11 countries would ratify the TPP, the TPP would not be effective without the ratification of the US.

of opportunity was small, since the battle for ratification was played in the final year of an outgoing presidency. Nonetheless, it was not an impossible task, if and only if the normal prevailed.

The battle for TPP ratification in 2016 was markedly different, compared to other trade agreement ratifications in the US. Globalists were outmatched by protectionists in terms of political leadership and also intellectual support.[54]

New tide of protectionism: This time is different

The rise of protectionism during election time is not something new in the US. We have seen it before. In the presidential race of 1992, Bill Clinton campaigned to renegotiate NAFTA. In the presidential race of 2008, Obama called the KORUS FTA unfair. Both candidates were from the Democratic Party.

But this time was different. Both presidential candidates spoke for protectionism. Surprisingly, the Republican Party turned its back on its long-held pro-trade stance. Trump's opposition to the TPP was something unheralded for the Presidential candidate from the Republican Party, which has been the mainstay of US leadership in global trade.

The two biggest trade agreements in the past two decades were initiated, negotiated, and concluded by Presidents from the Republican Party. It was

54 The following analysis is from Choi (2016) with some revision

George H.W. Bush who negotiated the NAFTA. It was his son, George W. Bush, who negotiated the KORUS FTA. In the past two Presidential elections, which elected and then re-elected Obama as President, each Presidential candidate from the Republican Party defended free trade. Trump broke this long-held pro-trade stance of the Republican Party.

The Democratic Party, which has been not so friendly to free trade, became more anti-trade in the name of fair trade. In 1993, 102 House Democrats cast "yes" vote for the NAFTA. In 2015, only 29 House Democrats supported the TPA request of President Obama. Despite virtually no chance for getting a nomination, Bernie Sanders stayed in the campaign race to the very end to press Hilary Clinton to accept his anti-TPP stance. Being pressed to the corner, Hilary Clinton withdrew her positive view of the TPP and was forced to be critical of the TPP.

The rise of Trump, the about-face of Hillary Clinton, and the surprising tenacity of Bernie Sanders were all related to the misfortunes of the middle and lower class in the US. Since the 1970s, the median real wage and real taxable income in the bottom 90% of the income distribution has seen no progress at all.[55] A gigantic gap has emerged and remained between the top 10% and the others since the early 1970s. Average real income in the bottom 90% was actually lower in 2013 than it was in 1972.[56] In previous elections, these people were less represented. But this time their anger and frustration found

55 Gordon (2016) p.605

56 Gordon (2016) p. 609-610

populistic outsiders in the name of Trump and Sanders. External and internal factors were at work behind the middle and lower class' economic misfortune. Somehow, external forces - international trade and immigration - got most of the blame. To understand why, we need to find what drives this new surge of protectionism.

Declining Intellectual Support for Free Trade: Elephant Curve

A conventional wisdom of globalization has is that "rising tide lifts all boats." Main stream economics has supported free trade on the grounds of "mutually beneficial transaction." The proposition was based on the comparison between two different situations for a national economy: before and after trade. The proof was a diagram showing that social welfare after trade would be bigger than social welfare before trade. In the big screen of university classroom all over the world, the picture was shown to incoming students year after year. Sure, there will be winners and losers. Those in import-competing sectors would face troubles due to intensifying competition with foreign imports. But no worries, because the market would work its wonders. Capital and workers in the losing sectors would be relocated into new sectors through the invisible hand of the market mechanism. The government would facilitate this reallocation process by absorbing initial trade shocks and offering job training programs. Everything considered, the gains from free trade outweigh the cost associated with free trade. The firm belief in free trade has been regarded as the article of faith for mainstream economists. This intellectual power has proved the bulwark against the rise of protectionism.

This time was different, though. Compared to the KORUS FTA and NAFTA, the intellectual support of the TPP was receding. Ardent intellectual support for globalism, which was instrumental in advancing international trade agreements against convicted opposition, became visibly in short supply. The ratification of the NAFTA in 1993 was a battle between the protectionists and the globalists. Against the protectionists' argument of job dislocation from the US to Mexico, the globalists countered: "more jobs and better jobs will be created in the US."[57] Back then, the job-creating argument was supported by mainstream economists. However, such undivided intellectual support for job creation became weaker over time. The intellectual pendulum has swung to the argument that trade produces so many painful job losses, which are not usually replaced by better jobs. The argument went further to claim that trade has caused the deepening of inequality. Milanovic and Lakner (2013) and Milanovic (2016) argued that people in the lower and middle parts of rich countries are "losers" from globalization, while the middle and upper classes of the relatively poor Asian countries and the global top 1% are "winners" from globalization, based on the global income distribution during 1988 to 2008. The graph showing the pattern was aptly named as the "Elephant Curve." In the political circle, the

57 When signing the NAFTA bill, President Clinton stated: "NAFTA means jobs. American jobs, and good-paying American jobs. If I didn't believe that, I wouldn't support this agreement."

Elephant Curve was regarded as the defining evidence of "rising tide lifts only some boats, not all boats," and in the context of the US, "rising tide lifts only yachts."

Some commentators interpreted the Elephant Curve as an evidence for the "globalization tradeoff": a hypothesis that economic growth of poor countries is achieved at the expense of the middle class in developed countries. This interpretation has developed popular notion that trading with poor countries is bad for the middle class in the US. For the 2016 presidential election campaign, the main target was China.

China Shock

Among the economics profession, the consensus was that trade had not been a major contributor to declining manufacturing employment or rising wage inequality in developed countries. Behind such consensus was the belief that workers in import-competing sectors could readily reallocate to other regions if displaced by trade; and aggregate gains from trade in the US would be positive even in the short-run or medium-run. Rise of China challenged such conventional wisdom.

With the accumulated data for the past 15 years or so, increasing number of papers and reports compiled negative effects of the Chinese import penetration to the US market, which was more disruptive than expected.[58]

58 Autor et al (2016)

Negative effects of job dislocation from trade prolonged. Negative distributional consequences were not small. Adjustment was not frictionless. The US had seen the surge of Japan in the 1970s and overcame that phenomenon. The surge of China, however, was considered to be different by the intellectual circle of the US. The sentiment of "China shock" is best summarized in an article of the Wall Street Journal: "No other country came close to its combination of a vast working-age population, super-low wages, government support, cheap currency and productivity gains."[59]

During 1979 to 2016, jobs in the US manufacturing sector have gone from 19 million to 12 million. Manufacturing jobs fluctuated around 18 million by 2000. Sharp decline began from 2001. During the period from 2000 to 2010, 5.6 million manufacturing jobs were lost. This is the largest decline in manufacturing employment in U.S. history. The sharp decline in American manufacturing employment began in 2001 just as Chinese imports took off. Political activists blame trade as the main culprit. Study of trade's impact on jobs is receiving growing attention among academic circles. The work of Autor, Dorn, and Hanson (2013) has made an interesting entry into this growing literature.[60] They estimate that a quarter of the US job loss in the manufacturing industry during 1990 to 2007 is due to imports from China. Pierce and Schott (2014) document the strong relation between the sharp

---

59 Davis and Hilsenrath (2016)

60 The growing literature in the study of China trade impact is found at http://chinashock.info/

decline in the US manufacturing industry since 2001 and the US conferral of PNTR on China, under which the US granted the MFN treatment to China like other WTO members.[61]

Conventional wisdom has been that technological change was more to blame. For instance, Hicks and Devaraj (2015) analyze that the job loss during 2000 to 2010 is largely accounted for by technology than by trade. Technological factor contributes to 85% of job loss, whereas trade factor contributes to 13.4%, according to their estimate. What has driven this transformation is the productivity increase. Hicks and Devaraj (2015) analysis delivers this point home. "Had we kept 2000-levels of productivity and applied them to 2010-levels of production, we would have required 20.9 million manufacturing workers. Instead, we employed only 12.1 million." Although the US manufacturing sector has experienced massive job loss since 2001, the productivity of the manufacturing sector has steadily increased.

This macro picture may miss the point, though. The estimate of Hicks and Devaraj (2015) shows that trade plays a bigger role in job loss in the sectors where import competition from developing countries, including China, is intense. In furniture and apparel sectors, the trade factor played more than 40 percent. Workers in these sectors are paid well below the wage of those in export sectors. In 2012, the average product of labor for all manufacturing was $149,299, from a low of $45,930 for manufacturers of

61 The US conferred this PNTR on China, when the US and China concluded China's accession negotiations to the WTO.

apparel and leather goods to $733,861 for petroleum and coal products manufacturing.[62]

Cheap imports have been lethal for many American manufacturers, particularly in the mid-Western rustbelt and in the south. The upsurge of protectionism in these regions is no coincidence at all. What is troublesome is that those workers in these sectors show the tendency of being trapped into a vicious circle. When they lose their jobs, they get another job in the same sector, and sooner or later find themselves in job search in the same sector again. This phenomenon is mainly due to their lack of proper skills or training to seek jobs in other sectors. Data reveals sharp rise in the college premium - the additional wages earned by more educated workers - from around 30% in 1979 to almost 50% by 2000.[63] Tracing the change of real weekly earnings by educational attainment during 1963-2012, Autor (2014) reports that the earning of those with a bachelor's degree and higher increased to 190, those with bachelor's degree saw their earnings increase to 140, but others fluctuated around 100-110.

The new tide of protectionism in the US cannot be fully appreciated without understanding the changing nature of intellectual debate on globalization and trade. These two undercurrents were closely related to and reinforced each other. Consequences were not just the defeat of the TPP on the domestic front. The election of Trump, a convinced protectionist,

---

62 Bureau of Labor Statistics, 2016

63 Bureau of Labor Statistics, 2016

as the new President was a seismic event in the waiting.

2. Emergence of the New Normal: Globalization without America[64]

Future historians would write the year 2016 as the time when the New Normal has finally arrived.[65] In 2016, the UK decided to withdraw from the EU ("Brexit"), and the US elected a convinced protectionist Trump as its next president. Both seismic events were loud declarations to the world that the two protagonists of the liberal international order would walk out of the stage. In retrospect, the Bretton Woods system of global economic architecture after World War II was the outcome of collaboration between the US and the UK. Their vision led to the creation of postwar liberal international order. In particular, in the area of international trade, the Trans-Atlantic collaboration between Washington and London has been more than instrumental to push and sustain the rule-based multilateral trading system against domestic opposition and unexpected external troubles. It is not exaggeration to state that the global expansion of the GATT/WTO was successful due to the Anglo-American leadership. After

64 The term of "Globalization without Normal" dates back to Choi (2017).

65 'New Normal' has been used to characterize something radically different pattern. 'New Normal' was used to refer the new economic circumstances in the wake of the 2008 global economic crisis. Chinese government also used 'New Normal' (新常態) in May 2014, when it tried to reset its policy direction from quantity to quality.

seven decades of spearheading, both the US and the UK decided to retreat from their leadership of providing the global public goods, and coincidentally at the same time!

Voting in free democracies renders opportunities for changing the incumbent leadership. In democratic societies where political apathy and sense of indifference run rampant, change through voting does not occur often. Usually, forces for change fall short on those for the status quo. When voting outcome directs for change, it means that the landscape has already transformed, and underneath currents have been radically shifted. What happened in the year 2016 was the manifestation of the sea change.

The heydays of free trade and rule-based multilateralism nexus are gone. In its place, result-oriented bilateralism is being vigorously promoted by the US. The new face of the New Normal is a new nexus of managed trade and power-based bilateralism. At the core, the New Normal is driven and reshaped by "Globalization without America." The election of Trump, who campaigned under the new mantra of "America First", "Buy American, Hire American," meant that the US would not shoulder the responsibility of offering and supporting global public goods beyond its stretch. Suddenly, the US, the architect and champion of Globalization, decided to walk away from the stage. With the exit of the US, liberal international order is under imminent threat.

The US has run substantial trade deficit with NAFTA members and Northeast Asian countries (Table 20). During the second Presidency of Obama, the US trade deficit with China and Korea have steadily increased.

This increasing bilateral trade deficit has been the main source of sharp criticism from Trump in the Presidential race of 2016. In the mindset of Trump, bilateral trade deficit meant unfair trade.

Table 20. US Trade Deficit in Merchandise Trade (US $ million)

	2012	2013	2014	2015	2016	Avg Rate %
Overall	741,171	702,587	741,462	759,307	736,794	-0.6%
China	315,103	318,713	343,079	365,695	347,016	10.1%
EU	116,383	125,557	142,058	153,318	146,760	26.1%
Canada	31,613	31,803	35,377	14,864	10,958	-65.3%
Mexico	61,719	54,485	53,825	58,364	64,354	4.3%
Japan	76,456	73,358	67,176	68,648	68,810	-10.0%
Korea	16,616	20,747	25,047	28,329	27,571	65.9%

**Source: US Census Bureau

3. New Nexus of Ideology-Institution-Technology

The emerging New Normal has an unfamiliar nexus of ideology -institution-technology as its core element. Under the New Normal, there is no place for the US in the driver seat of advancing globalization and maintaining the liberal international order. The US declared retreat from the universe it designed and championed for the seven decades since World War II. China, the rising powerful state, is poised to fill in the leadership vacuum. President Xi's speech in Davos 2017 is China's triumphant declaration to the world: "Now, only China can save free trade." However, the truth is far from it. Xi's laudable words need to be implemented. Action speaks louder than words. While China is hesitant in embarking on its promised reform, Chinese trade sanctions on Korean products in relation to THAAD serve a vivid example of the shadow of overstretching China. The belief that free and open trade would promote prosperity and peace is disappearing. In its place, reciprocal and fair trade is promoted by the US. Using its power and influence, the new US intends to transform rule-based free trade to power-based managed trade.

The post-Cold War trade-security nexus, under which trade expansion would promote peace among different political regimes, is about to be replaced by a new trade-security nexus. The so-called "Golden Arches Theory of Conflict Prevention" - that two countries with a McDonalds would not go to war - will be no longer the case.[66] Positive externalities to security from increased trade would not be there anymore. In the Old Normal, trade disputes among allies were resolved within the context of trade policy. They were not much politicized. Only in trade disputes with non-allies, security concerns often overrode trade issues. In some high profile cases, security was offered as excuse for trade sanction. When it comes to trade disputes among allies, however, there were confidence and trust among policymakers from allies that the security of allies would not be impaired, even if trade disputes became too serious to be resolved. In the New Normal, such a conventional firewall between trade and security

66 Friedman (1998)

among allies seems awry.

The New Normal was at vivid display when the US resorted to national security concern to reduce its import of steel and aluminum in March 2018. Based on a year-long investigation and recommendations by the Department of Commerce, President Trump decided to impose tariffs on steel (25%) and aluminum (10%) in March 2018, invoking Section 232 of the US Trade Expansion Act of 1962. The EU, Canada, Mexico, Korea, and Japan, which are allies of the US, were included in the hit list, along with China and other countries. Trade Expansion Act of 1962, and Section 232 (Security Exception) were the legacy of the Cold War. Even during the Cold War era, Section 232 were rarely used against non-allies.

The arrival of President Trump to the power revived Section 232 from the dust. The US intends to invoke 'Security Exception' of Section 232 to change the rule-based global trading system. When he announced the imposition of tariffs on steel and aluminum, President Trump indicated the US willingness to negotiate bilaterally with countries on the hit list. From strategic point of view, what he is doing is a classic posture to create negotiating leverage. From the past negotiations at the GATT/WTO, the US agreed to tariffs on steel and aluminum. The US bound tariffs for aluminum and aluminum products are 5.7 percent and below. For steel the US bound rates range from zero to 12.5 percent, with the overwhelming majority of tariff lines bound at 5 percent or below. Taking these as ceiling, in practice the US has been imposing lower tariffs on MFN-basis. As for steel, typical applied tariffs were less than 6%.[67] What the US is trying to do by invoking Section 232 is to threaten to raise tariffs above the bound level.

This attempt has serious negative impacts on the rule-based global trading system. In its attempts to reduce chronic trade deficits on the products of which security linkage is doubtful, President Trump completely ignores the existing global trading system of the WTO. He exempted Canada and Mexico at least temporarily, under the excuse of on-going NAFTA renegotiations. The same standard was not applied to Korea, even though the KORUS renegotiations were also under way. Negotiating outcome varies. Korea was exempted from 25% tariffs on steel in return for its acceptance of quota (70% of the annual average Korean steel exports to the US over the past three years: 2015-2017).[68] Quota is prohibited in the WTO, which the US championed to create and strengthen. Now, the US demanded quota to Korea to reduce Korea's steel export to the US in the name of security concern.

Under so-called "fair and reciprocal" trade policy of Trump, different tariffs level, not MFN, and different terms of market access to the US would be applied to different countries, as the unfolding case of steel exemplifies. Korea exports only up to 70% level of years 2015-2017. No more than that level, even though some Korean companies are willing to export by accepting high tariffs of 25%. While Korea compromised for 70% quota, some country agreed on different quota. Argentina agreed to limit exports

67 Numbers are from the WTO database.

68 USTR (2018)

of steel products to the US to 180,000 tons per year, based on the average of steel exports during the past three years plus an additional 35%, in return for exemption from 25% tariff imposed on steel. Countries which would not compromise with the US would face 25% tariffs for their steel export to the US. Hence, different market access condition for different countries, driven by the yardstick of the US! This outcome is precisely what the reciprocal trade is trying to achieve.

The US, the very architect and the largest stakeholder of the rule-based multilateral trading system, has turned inward, as the slogan of "America First" says it all. Under President Trump, the US would seek its domestic interest, including sectoral interest of declining industry (often called as the Rust Belt) disadvantaged from international competition, at the expense of the established global norm. President Trump seems not intent to preserve interest of alliance. He threatened to terminate the NAFTA and the KORUS, unless existing free trade agreements would not be renegotiated and amen ded to the favorable terms of the US domestic interest. President Trump's perception of allies is revealed when he said: "We are going to charge countries that take advantage of the US, some of them are our so-called allies but they're not allies on trade."[69]

Due to changing ideology of the US, multilateralism is in complete disarray. The WTO has already become incompetent and ineffective, and

69 https://www.realclearpolitics.com/video/2018/02/12/trumpso-called_allies_are_not_alies_on_trade_we_are_going_to_charge_reciprocal_tax.html

now under the danger of becoming irrelevant. With the demise of the WTO, the global trading system is in the midst of a transitional crisis. The growing concern is that the US has begun its effort to change the WTO, if it would not attempt to desert or destroy it. The US will cease to have multilateral institutions as its main stay. Instead, it will resort to bilateralism. The new mantra of "reciprocal and fair trade" will replace "free and open trade."

New Normal finds its company in the new technological landscape. In the past, the ICT helped to shape and strengthen the GVC. Due to the ICT which tremendously reduced the communication cost of carrying ideas, an increasing number of companies have gone global. Each segment of production process from a drawing board to the hands of consumers has found its proper location in the world, pursuant to company's strategy. As analyzed in Chapter 2, the ICT played a role of "integrating technology" for globalization.

On the other hand, the current wave of digital transformation, often called as the Fourth Industrial Revolution, promises the complete disruption of economic activities and organization of tasks. Conventional organization of production network on the globe is in danger of severe disruption. In this sense, on-going technological breakthrough is "disruptive technology". An example may serve the point well. The US President Obama was anxious to bring manufacturing jobs back to the US. During his presidency, the US pursued the "Business U-Turn" policy. Out of his desire to restore American business, Obama asked Steve Jobs, the then-CEO of Apple, "What would it take to make iPhones in the United States?" Almost all of the 70 million iPhones, 30 million iPads and 59 million other products Apple sold in the previous year (2011) were manufactured overseas. Jobs' reply was unambiguous. "Those jobs aren't coming back."[70]

In the era of digital transformation, American-made iPhone is no longer a political agenda. It can be a viable business strategy. The advance of digital economy would make Obama's desire as reality, but with a twist. Perhaps jobs may not come back. In smart factories located somewhere in the US, assembly of iPhone will be done by robots and Artificial Intelligence (AI). Reshoring will not have to find its way on populism, but on the new technological landscape.

In the light of all these changes in Ideology and Technology, the existing Ideology-Institution-Technology Nexus as depicted in Chapter 2 (Figure 4) is being replaced by New Normal, as illustrated in Figure 8 and Table 21.

Figure 8. Ideology-Institution-Technology Nexus under New Normal

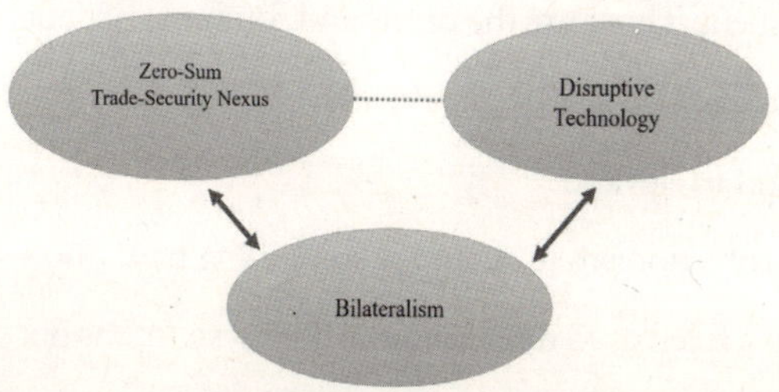

**Source: Author's illustration

70 Duhigg and Bradsher (2012).

Table 21. Old Normal vs New Normal: Ideology-Institution-Technology Nexus

	Old Normal	New Normal
Trade-security nexus	positive-sum	zero-sum
Technology	Integrating technology	Disruptive technology
Institution	Rule-based multilateralism	Power-based bilateralism

**Source: Author's own

4. Implications of the New Normal to Northeast Asia

Weak Institutionalization: WTO in Disarray

China, Japan, and Korea are all active members of the multilateral trading system. Japan and Korea have joined the GATT and became the founding members of the WTO. China joined the WTO in 2001. As members of the WTO, the three countries are given non-discriminatory access (MFN and NT) to other members' market. In case of trade disputes, they could bring their complaints to the WTO and rely on its established mechanism of dispute settlement. Those are the prime and foremost benefits of the WTO. However, increasingly and visibly, the WTO became incompetent, ineffective, and irrelevant.

Rise of protectionism itself is not something new. Success of free and open trade on a rule-based multilateral trading system was not given for free. It was earned through fights. More often than not, inward-looking nationalism surfaced. Each time, free traders rose to the occasion, and multilateralism became strengthened. Recurrence of crisis on the global scale such as the 1970s oil shocks, the 1980s recession, and the 1990s Asian financial crisis led to the surfacing of protectionism and economic nationalism. Each time, US political leadership rose to the challenge. The completion of the Tokyo Round and the Uruguay Round was only possible due to the US, which put the integrity of rule-based free and open trade ahead of its myopic national interest. These efforts gave rise to the bicycle theory of trade liberalization: "Keep pedaling or you fall off."

Seventeen years of negotiations could not complete the DDA. The DDA negotiations have become the longest running trade talks ever. So far, the DDA negotiations have taken twice the time than the previous Uruguay Round, and is still far from going through the finish line. The chance of successful completion has long gone. Members of the WTO are divided on a pathway. The US and EU delivered a death sentence to the DDA in the Nairobi gathering of the WTO trade ministers. They proposed that the WTO should adopt a new modus operandi, instead of a single undertaking approach (negotiating all agenda until agreement is found). Other members opposed, because it would wreck the multilateral trading system. But for a single undertaking approach, they assert, balance of trade negotiations would be critically tilted to the advantage of powerful countries.

The dispute settlement mechanism of the WTO faces imminent danger of unravelling. For some years, the US has been taking a critical stance on the operations of the WTO's Appellate Body (AB), which composes of seven standing members. For each appealed case, three members are assigned by the WTO agreement. Each AB member serves four-year term, which may be renewed for another four-year term. After serving two terms, the member should leave the AB, and the WTO searches for a new member. The US has been blocking the selection of new AB members. As a result, three vacancies on the seven-member body have not been filled.

What drives the US stubborn objection in this case? The US argues that the WTO dispute settlement system has gone out of its way to the point of making a new trade agreement by itself. In a speech during the 2017 Buenos Aires WTO Ministerial Conference, US Trade Representative Robert Lighthizer claimed:

> *"The WTO is losing its essential focus on negotiation and becoming a litigation-centered organization. Too often members seem to believe they can gain concessions through lawsuits that they could never get at the negotiating table. We have to ask ourselves whether this is good for the institution and whether the current litigation structure makes sense."*[71]

What would be the consequence of US insistence? It may lead to a bizarre situation where the AB ceases to function. Unless new AB members are appointed, the AB will face severe delays. If the number of AB members is down to two, the AB could not operate, since each case requires at least three sitting judges. This could lead to an extreme scenario of the crumbling

---

71 Opening Plenary Statement of USTR Robert Lighthizer at the WTO Ministerial Conference 2017. Lighthizer went on to warn that the US would have to consider taking action if the WTO finds in China's favor in a dispute over whether China deserves "market economy" status in the WTO. There has been criticism of the WTO's institutional capacity to cope with a rising China.

of the WTO dispute settlement system.

In addition to the incompetence and ineffectiveness of the WTO system, the WTO is in danger of becoming irrelevant. The WTO agreement is mainly on the flow of goods and services. The current WTO agreement reflects the economic realities of the 1990s. The global economy has moved on since then. The landscape of global economy is so radically different from those days. The ICT revolution, which swept through the 1990s and the beginning of the new millennium, the emergence of the GVC, the rise of the Digital Economy, and the rise of China have all brought new challenges to the WTO. Issues resulting from these developments, such as E-commerce, Labor and Trade, Environment and Trade, and State Owned Enterprise (SOE) are so critical to the global trading system, but are largely outside of the scope of the WTO.

China going-it-alone

Incompetent, ineffective, and irrelevant WTO is ill-suited for navigating the turbulent global economy. The visible continuous weakening in the WTO system is the outcome of growing hostility between the declining US and the rising, and assertive, China, and their failure to resolve differences.

The New Normal is a consequence of the US changing its approach to confront the rise of assertive China. Naturally the great ramification of the New Normal is felt in Northeast Asia. China is no longer just cheap China. China has heavy and chemical industries with unprecedented scale of capacities, which compete with Japan and Korea head on. In the aftermath of the 2008 Global Economic Crisis, the excess capacity has presented a major issue for global coordination. Despite dire necessity for coordinated reduction of excess capacity, China had refused to act. Compared to Japan and Korea, where those capacities are at the hands of private firms, China's capacity is at the hands of SOE. The strategy of Beijing is to maintain excess capacity and play the war of attrition in the hope that other countries' firms would give in. Once the dust settles, Beijing reckons, China will emerge as the winner.

Another worrisome development is the growing appetite of Beijing to ignore the standard rule of the game. It has been widely reported that foreign firms in China are discriminated compared to local ones, forced to transfer technology, blocked from competition, and exposed to constant threat of theft of intellectual properties. In a glaring example, two Korean companies, which are assessed to be at the forefront of battery for electric car, have been virtually out of the business in China due to flip-flop regulatory changes of the Chinese government. These companies were allured to China by the promise of production subsidy for electric car battery. Once in China, they found that the Chinese authority was unwilling to provide subsidy to them. Upon their protest, the Chinese government changed regulations so that the Korean companies were ineligible for subsidy. Years of preparation for investment, and all those capital invested in China of these Korean firms were wasted. They are now fearful of forced technology transfer to local Chinese firms as condition for subsidy.

Made in China 2025: Nationalism without brake

When Beijing announced the Made in China 2025 strategy in 2015, China unveiled its ambition of leapfrogging, not catch-up, and joining the ranks of major manufacturing powers. Made in China 2025 tries to emulate the Industry 4.0 of Germany, the vision of smart, efficient, and fully-networked manufacturing wherein sophisticated technologies help integrate production, suppliers, business partners, and customers. Remarks of Premier Li Keqiang summed up the ambition behind the initiative: "We will implement the 'Made in China 2025' strategy, seek innovation-driven development, apply smart technologies, strengthen foundations, pursue green development, and redouble our efforts to upgrade China from a manufacturer of quantity to one of quality."

Made in China 2025 is also China's ambitious blueprint for changing its global image. For quite some time, the term of Made in China has been associated with negative connotation - cheap, poor quality, and fake. As the second largest economy in the world on the verge of overtaking the US, China wanted to change such a negative image. Clearly, China's manufacturing sector needs a push to take it to the next level, and this is where Made in China 2025 comes in. According to the government's action plan, China will aim for a big leap in innovation as well as manufacturing efficiency, and realize basic industrialization by 2025; be able to compete with developed manufacturing powers by 2035; and lead the world's manufacturing industry by the 100th birthday (2049) of the New China. The plan will focus more on high-tech industries such as Information Technology, Robotics,

Aerospace, and New Materials.

China's transformation is based on its unfair treatment of foreign companies, to the eyes of foreign business in China. They claim that "Made in China 2025," an ambitious 10-year government plan designed to boost innovation in manufacturing, is "just another excuse for protectionism." Made in China 2025 blueprint mentions "strengthened security reviews" for investments, mergers and acquisitions, and procurement in manufacturing areas related to the national economy and national security, which are not clearly defined. Language in the Made in China 2025 plan also seeks to boost indigenous innovation. For example, it lists the goal of ensuring that domestic Chinese firms will handle the majority of local infrastructure development with specific timetables. For example, the plan states that 40% of core infrastructure components and key infrastructure materials should come from Chinese sources by 2020 and increased further to 80% by 2025. This has led to concerns that foreign firms would be discriminated under the plan.

Made in China 2025 Initiative is, in fact, a bold statement for aggressive industrial policy. Foreign firms would be ill equipped to meet the challenges, as seen in the saga of the Korean electric car battery manufacturing companies in China. Made in China 2025 is not the one and only thorny issue in the era of the New Normal. The list runs quite long. China's growing appetite of acquiring foreign technologies through aggressive M&A in the global stage, mainly in the US, has already touched off alarm bells. The list goes on to Beijing's stubborn and relentless repression on cyberspace, mandatory requirement of technology transfer as condition for investing in China, alleged theft of technology and violation of intellectual property right, and so on.

The future course of China under the New Normal is a major concern for Korea and Japan. Conventional trade ties would not guarantee stability any more, as the THAAD-related trade sanctions attest. Slowdown of economic growth and assertive China may be a deadly combination. Despite its pledges, Beijing has less stomach for steadfast reform of its vulnerable SOE, financial sector, and overcapacity. In Northeast Asia, the contest is not between varieties of capitalism, but between state capitalism and market capitalism. Chinese-style state capitalism has deftly managed to overcome the crises of 1997 and 2008. It learned how to survive and outlive. Its emboldened decisiveness makes its neighbors uncomfortable. Without securing an effective coordination mechanism to work with Beijing, Seoul and Tokyo will be in trouble. This is the newly emerging landscape of New Normal in Northeast Asia.

The emergence of the New Normal means inward-looking economic nationalism and populism on the rise. The US is turning inward, putting domestic constituency ahead of global interest. The UK, which has accompanied the US in creating and strengthening the Old Normal, has turned inward. China is unabashedly going at it alone, paying less attention to the global norm. Rule-based multilateralism is in disarray. The WTO has been sidelined and would not be relied on to mediate major disputes. G20, which proved instrumental in preventing the 2008 global crisis from exploding to the 21st Great Depression, lost its magic.

What took place at the G20 Summit in 2017 illustrates the emergence of New Normal. In Hamburg, G20 leaders could not denounce agree on the unconditional opposition to protectionism, which they had been doing in previous summits. Just a year ago in Hangzhou G20 Summit in 2016, leaders agreed on the language of "We reiterate our opposition to protectionism on trade and investment in all its forms."[72] Back then, the US was represented by President Obama.

At the 2017 Hamburg G20 Summit, the language G20 leaders negotiated and agreed on was: "We will keep markets open noting the importance of reciprocal and mutually advantageous trade and investment frameworks and the principle of non-discrimination, and continue to fight protectionism including all unfair trade practices and recognize the role of legitimate trade defense instruments. We will strive to ensure a level playing field, in particular by promoting a favorable environment for trade and investment"[73] (some omission by the author)

While they still mentioned "fighting protectionism", new emphasis was on 'reciprocal and mutually advantageous' trade and investment framework, and "level playing field". "Fair and reciprocal" trade, the hallmark of Trump trade policy, made forceful entry to the G20. The G20 Summit in 2017

72 G20 leaders' communique, Hangzhou summit, 4-5 September 2016.

73 "G20 Leaders' Declaration - Shaping an interconnected world"

witnessed the beginning of the end of Old Normal, and the emergence of New Normal. With the familiar cover of Old Normal, middle and small-power countries have hard time trying to figure out survival tactics. To add insult to injury, on-going digital revolution disrupts conventional GVC. Not before long, securing assembly task out of the production process of the products with global brand would not ensure a fighting chance for joining the industrialized world in the era of digital transformation. Although the case for more effective global coordination to make the most of the potential and to reduce disruption of on-going technological breakthrough is strong and urgent, both the leading power and the emerging power are not willing to exercise the global leadership.

6 Undercurrent, Risk, and Strategic Imperative

1. China Question

In projecting the future of Northeast Asia, China holds a key to the crystal ball. As a risen regional power, the ambition, mindset, and strategy of China will influence the shape of the first-order issue of security and prosperity of the region and all other second-order issues such as environment and energy. For the very question of the future of China, the most essential and fundamental question is: Can China keep it going without changing its political system? More precisely, can China keep moving up the ladder of growth and achieves inclusive growth without changing its political system of the Communist Party dictatorship?

Since its turn to the reform and opening back to 1978, the Chinese communist state has found its legitimacy from high-flying economic growth. Dramatic and sustained economic growth has lifted the Chinese from the poverty, created non-farming jobs, and enhanced the living standard. After three decades of high-flying, the Chinese economy is hitting the wall. The wall of so-called "regression to the mean." The idea is that an economy cannot keep performing high rate of growths indefinitely. At an early stage of economic development, simply working more hours and building more factories would generate modest growth. Working longer hours by more and more workers in conjunction with more and more new production facilities would lead to high growth. This phase, however, would come to an end. There is limit to the maximum workable hours and the size of total workers. Production facilities cannot be installed indefinitely. Economic law of diminishing return to scale would bite them eventually. Any heated economy would slow down sooner or later.

Throughout history, a spurt of sudden high growth episodes was followed by sudden slow down or even collapse. The case of Japan falls in the second category. "Lost Decades" is the term used for describing the remarkable lapse of growth after dramatic rise to the point of overtaking the US as the largest economy. On-going drama of Korea is believed to be in the first category. The Korean economic growth in the 21st century has been below the global average. An economy dubbed as the second Japan, in terms of growth pattern and speed, seems losing the memory of growing up. What is common between Japan and Korea is both countries failed to transform their system. Japan had not embarked on deep reform.

Despite its world-class manufacturing, its financial system was subpar and its market was virtually closed to the global imports. Competition was restrained, innovation was incremental, and the country built the regulatory barriers against foreign access to its market. Japan failed to translate its economic power into the source for the next horizon. Reasons behind sudden slowdown of the Korean economy are not much different. In both countries, deep reforms were not seriously embarked on. The logic of regression to the mean implies that a country needs to transform its system through deep reform, if it wants to avoid the path down to slow down.

It has been argued that China is not exception to this regression to the mean. Slow-down of the Chinese economy from its 8 percent annual growth rate to 6 percent is not surprising. Rather, it is even natural. Regression to the mean predicts the growth rate would continue to move down. The question is the speed of slowing down. China watchers have been debating about how long China can keep performing 6 percent growth rate. Even after three decades of almost 10 percent of annual growth, China is still thirsty for high growth. In order to address thorny issues such as inequality, environment, social safety net, and welfare system, which threaten the legitimacy of the authoritarian regime of the Chinese Communist Party, at least 6 percent growth should be maintained for some time. Lower growth rate means lesser jobs, less income increase, less government budget for infrastructure upgrading and welfare spending.

Conventional wisdom, which is also the mainstream view, is that deep reform is imperative for China. Reforms on the financial sector and the SOE, among others, are priorities. These are Achilles heel of the Chinese political economic system, and also the very area where the grip of the government is still strong. Delayed reform in these sectors would mean the inefficient scare resource allocation, which will spell inefficiency and corruption.

Regulatory risks would impede the smooth business operation of local and foreign investors. In particular, foreign investors in China without deep reforms would be in the danger of being trapped. Government may interfere anytime at its discretion. Doing business under this precarious situation is like carrying explosives.

Some argue that the case for reform is exaggerated. They assert that the lapse of reform in the financial sector and the SOE is not unique problem, confined to China alone. They turn to the fact that advanced democratic countries also have SOEs and the financial sector under strong regulation. Such argument misses critical point. Whilst it is true that some advanced democratic countries maintain rather stringent financial regulations and some SOE, they are subject to the regulatory oversight and, equally important, check and balance of political system, the free press, and the vigilant civil society. China does not possess any of these critical elements for transparent and predictable system.

Contending views

At the present, the two diametrically-opposed views are being contested:

View A : China will face the end of its rise without deep reform.

View B : China will continue to move ahead regardless of deep reform.

View A finds its ardent supporters in the usual suspects of the Western scholars, public intellectuals, media and politicians. Although some differences in their tone and nuance, they are skeptical of the future of China. In their analysis, China will not undertake deep reform, because deep reform is tantamount to transfer of the power of Communist Party to the market. Insecure power elite of Beijing will not take such a bold gamble. Their prediction is that China will hit the wall before long. The end outcome will be China in middle income trap, or prolonged recession, or even worse future.

Within View A, in fact two discernable views exist. View A1 take the fundamentalist approach. The proponents of this view argue that there will not be economic reform without political reform, no economic reform. They go on to assert that chance for political reform is little due to fear of instability This drastic view predicts the demise of the Communist China as we have known. Minxin Pei and David Shambaugh are leading proponents of this view. They readily point out that the implementation record of so-much heralded 2013 reform blueprint is not up to the initial hype. As a matter of fact, assessment reports as prepared by foreign entities with high stakes in China are critical about lack of much progress. Quick reference to the latest US-China Business Council report and the European Chamber of Commerce in China (ECCC) would attest disappointment. Prevailing sentiment among China watchers is that most of reform pledges still remain on the document, despite some positive steps.

A less fatalistic, but yet critical view, A2, is also offered. They assert that China will be forced to undertake reform, because there is no alternative.

Barry Naughton (2016) represented View A2 succinctly:

"*The pressures pushing toward more profound reform are very strong. For, at the end of the day, the reformers are right: only major institutional changes that make the economy more open, competitive, and rules-bound can avoid the serious problems that otherwise loom. . China must continue economic reforms in order to become a technologically creative and institutionally flexible economy with a high standard of living for a majority of its citizens.*"

On the other hand, View B argues that regardless of the implementation of deep reform, China has already moved on to the New Economy. Within View B, two differentiated views are observed. View B1 is "Pragmatic optimism", which argues that China has successfully transformed itself as new Digital power house. They draw their case on the thriving mobile economy, Chinese mobile giants such as Alibaba, Baidu, and Tencent, and the rise of Shenzen as the silicon valley of Asia. A new group of Chinese entrepreneurs with global reach is also their favorite reference.

Another View B2 takes a strong dose of nationalistic optimism. According to this view, China will continue to rise, will deal with obstacles, due to its pragmatism, and the party leadership has proved other sceptics (mainly Western) wrong. This "China is different" view is in the wide circulation among the Chinese scholars with global contact. They seem to heavily rely on the past experience of China's astonishing continued growth path, irrespective of half-hearted implementation of liberalization, deregulation and privatization. According to them, China proved wrong the western conventional wisdom, and China will prove them wrong again. Proponents of View B2 argue that the idea of deep reform is a typical

Western bias of pro-market neo-liberalism. They went on to assert that deep reform is the Western conspiracy to instill the seeds of destroying the Chinese communist regime.

China in Halfway House

A minimum level of deep reform requires the establishment of independent regulatory oversight without interference from the Chinese Communist Party. Such a regulatory system will have built-in due processes applicable to all stakeholders, domestic and foreign. It would help advance rule-based decision making, not decisions made by whims and discretion of the Communist Party. Such an act would promote more vibrant and dynamic economic activities, which are essential for the transformation of China from quantity to quality. As long as this step is not undertaken, the market would get the signal that all those talks and documents on reform are just empty rhetoric.

Both views tend to be extreme. Deep reform has a certain Western bias, while the other view is too much colored with nationalistic tone. Both views show lack of understanding of the operation of the state and the market in deeply embedded cultural context. More realistic prognosis would be China in the halfway house. To understand and project China's move, one needs to place her analysis in the context of history.[74]

74 Approach from this perspective is found, for instance, in Huang (2017).

In its first stage of opening up, out of dire necessity, China welcomed foreign investment. Foreign investors were not just provider of scarce capital and the job creator. They were teachers. China learned how to organize production activities and run business as on-going concern, and create industry. As a consequence, Factory China emerged and moved on to its expansionary phase. The success of Factory China spelled the rise of China. With the advance of Factory China, the Chinese local industry began to emerge and slowly placed its name in the global map. During this stage, the relationship with foreign investors changed from lopsided for foreigners to more or less even. Now, ambition of China has grown bigger than its economic realities. It wants to overtake and leapfrog foreign firms globally, not just in its home market.

State capitalism of China as called by the Western world misses an important point. China learned how to use the market when it finds necessary. China also got lesson of not to overstretch too much too premature. To the Chinese intellectuals and power elites, the case of the 1997 Asian Financial Crisis, in particular the case of Korea, reminds the danger of opening up too much pursuant to the Western request. Whether right or wrong, they got the impression that the financial opening up would invite Trojan horse.

Many Western experts and policy makers presumed that accumulated inefficiency of China, mainly debt, would necessitate China's reform measures. Chinese policy makers were fully recognizant of the seriousness of the trouble. In 2007, Premier Wen Jiabao called the Chinese economy "unstable, unbalanced, uncoordinated, and unsustainable." Contrary to Western expectations, however, the choice taken by China was not opening up for greater competition and accompanying reform. China's opening up and liberalization has been stalled since the early years of the 21st century. Its membership in the WTO and the pursuit of the WTO did not translate into more and deep opening. China has doubled down its effort to scale up its SOEs and grips on the financial system.

Instead of opening up to the outside world, China turned inside. China decided to stay on its course of consolidating SOEs and promoting local firms through strong control of finance. China became even more bold and determined. China's blueprint of Made in China 2025 is in every detail the industrial policy redux. Relying on protection, promotion, and discrimination, China aims to promote national champions in critical technology sectors including aerospace, biomedicine, and robotics. Foreign firms will have less space to compete with Chinse ones. The playing field will never be level for foreign firms in China.

President Xi Jinping's first five-year term ended in 2017. In the 19th Party Congress in October 2017, Xi secured another five-year term until 2022. After the Congress, several China watchers came to the projection that "Xi's rule is now set to last for the next 15 years and perhaps beyond." Such projection proved to be reality, when in March 2018 China removed the term limit for its top leader. Extended power of Xi would set China in the uncharted course for the third decade of the 21st century. Shared consensus among China watchers is that the Communist Party felt so insecure due to the growing signs of dissatisfaction in the hinterland and from farmers moved to urban area, that they threw their support to Xi so that he could stabilize the country.

China under the consolidated and strong leadership may continue to suppress political freedom. Political repression alone would not achieve the goal of the Chinese Dream. Chinese economy needs more sustained growth. The second biggest economy on its way to become the largest economy cannot keep it up unless it maintains a certain degree of ties to the global flow of products, capital, ideas, and people. Just looking inward and blocking foreign entry to the Chinese market would not make China stronger and effective. Absence of reform in the financial sector and the SOE will backfire. At the same time, deep reform would be risky. The already insecure Communist Party would feel the existential threat in case the private sector and the market become too powerful and overtake the Communist Party.

The challenge of Xi Jinping, who is likely to stay in power beyond 2023 due to the recent elimination of term limit, is to take a balancing act. He is caught between the Marxist leftist and the reform-minded. The leftist contend that growing and severe inequality is hurting the vision of the Communist society, and further Western influence into China should not be tolerated. The rightest claim that more alignment with the global economy is necessary for China's pursuit of rich and powerful country, and reform is an essential step. The leftist is of the view that enough is enough, while the other side believes that we should not stop here. Despite their apparent irreconcilable difference, one thing that both sides can agree on is wishing to maintain the solidarity and firm security of the Communist Party.

In this perspective, deep reform is not the most burning issue in the mindset of the Chinese leadership under President Xi. As a priority, President Xi will resolve the debt problem, and take care of inequality and the environmental degradation. The Communist Party leadership is fearful of another moment like the 1989 Tiananmen pro-democracy protest. If President Xi is successful in managing these urgent problems, both the left and the right would continue to support him. As its next step, China will slowly, and often grudgingly, show intermittent attempts of changing its financial system and the SOEs. The speed and the scope would be to some extent decided through the interplay between China's and the foreign countries' grand strategy and negotiations.

In this contest, China's global ambition to globalize its currency may play a role. When China's yuan joined the IMF's basket of reserve currencies in 2016, it was the acceptance of China's growing economic power. Though such an event was a milestone for Beijing's march in the global power map, achieving the status of global currency like the US dollar, the Euro, and the Japanese yen would require the Chinese government to loosen its grip on the financial system and establish a new and globally acceptable system. Freely-floating currency market and currency market freely accessible to foreigners are essential components of the global system. So far, no local currency has gained the status of global currency without convertibility and with a closed financial sector to foreigners. The current situation of China is far and away from this end point. China would try to achieve such a status without losing its strong grip. The incumbent of the global financial system would not make that happen. China's fighting chance looks slim at the present. If China continues to surge, then who knows? The race is on.

2. Changing Ideological Landscape in Northeast Asia

China increasingly turning to Nationalism

Since Xi got the power in 2012, China gradually distanced itself from the US-led global architecture and became confrontational. The Belt Road Initiative is the first incarnation of China's global ambition. It is designed to counter the US-led TPP. Establishing the AIIB is the second move in the geopolitical grand strategy of China. On-going dispute on the South China Sea is showing a defiant, yet confident face of China. The biggest beneficiary of the West-led globalization, China has turned to left-wing nationalism, of which legitimacy is sought in rectifying 150 years of humiliation.[75] At the same time, new ideology is also populistic, firmly rooted in the egalitarian vision of the Chinese Communist Party. The vision of Chinese Dream is the culmination of left-wing nationalism in the clothes of populism.

In 2012, President Xi unveiled the vision of the Chinese Dream. Xi stated, "The Chinese Dream is the great rejuvenation of the Chinese

---

75 The leaked internal memo of the Chinese Communist Party, known as Document No. 9, warned the Western democracy as a plot to weaken, destabilize, and eventually break up China. (China File 2013)

nation." Xi's Chinese Dream is to accomplish two goals: the material goal of China becoming a "moderately well-off society" by 2021, and the modernization goal of China becoming a fully developed nation by 2049.

China did not throw away the cover of globalism all together. China will continue to play the globalism card, as long as it is in the interest of China. Access to the global market spelled the rise of China from a poor agrarian economy to a developing manufacturing economy. From now on, access to global technology would spell the Chinese Dream to the status of a developed innovative economy. In its strive for the Chinese dream, Beijing intends to play the game by its own rule, not by the so-called global rules. For the Chinese power elites, globalism will increasingly be a convenient cover. They will turn to globalism whenever they feel necessary.

In fact, even after its dramatic switch to reform and opening up in 1978, nationalism and populism have been deep inside China. China became pragmatic enough to take advantage of globalization, while suppressing and hiding the temptation for nationalism and populism. When the world started to observe the "assertive" face of China, innate true colors of China have at last surfaced.

Where have those reform-minded globalists gone? Are they becoming an endangered species? Or have they decided to hide their identities due to the headwinds of rising anti-globalism? Sooner or later, China will confront moments of truth. Its fulfillment of the Chinese Dream will not be a smooth ride. Various risks, internal and external, foreseen and unforeseen, will test leadership. Those testing times will witness clashes of ideological fault lines.

In times of crisis, the strong case for globalism, outnumbered at the moment, will be growing.

Japan trying to find hope in Globalism

After the prolonged depression, called as "Lost Decades", Japan is trying hard to rekindle economic dynamism. Under the leadership of Prime Minister Abe, one of the longest running Prime Minister in post-war Japan, Japan turned around the corner. Two noteworthy changes are visible. They are making great impacts in the geopolitical landscape of Northeast Asia.

In the rising tide of the New Normal, Japan finds itself in closer alignment with the US when it comes to addressing China and North Korea. At the first glance, it looks paradoxical. Because the new US under President Trump broke down the TPP, the very core element of renewed Japan-US alliance, which had been shaped through Obama-Abe diplomacy. On second thought, it is only reasonable. Inherently Japan sought its place in the global stage in closer coordination with the US. The post-war Japanese diplomacy was in essence following the US lead and cue. Henceforth, Japan's global power was uni-directional, even though Japan had grown to the second largest economy in the world. Japan's economic power did not translate into other dimensions. It was not by choice. It was due to constraints.

The constitution of Japan, which was compromised between the victorious Allied Power, in fact the US, and the defeated Japan, deprived Japan of the power to attack other countries. Titled as "Renunciation of War,"

Article 9 states:

> *Aspiring sincerely to an international peace based on justice and order, the Japanese people forever renounce war as a sovereign right of the nation and the threat or use of force as means of settling international disputes. In order to accomplish the aim of the preceding paragraph, land, sea, and air forces, as well as other war potential, will never be maintained. The right of belligerency of the state will not be recognized.*

Article 9 stipulates that Japan renounces its right to wage war. The intention behind Article 9 was to replace Japan's imperial military regime to liberal democracy. In return for the so-called "Peace constitution," the US promised to provide military and nuclear protection. Prime Minister Abe aims to change Article 9 of the Peace Constitution. Japan is thrown into a domestic battle between right-wing nationalism and globalism. Those arguing for the change of the constitution base their argument on the rise of assertive China, which poses a major threat to the sovereignty of Japan. North Korea's growing nuclear ambition added more urgency and potency to their argument. On the other hand, globalists in Japan counter that the change of the Peace Constitution would put Japan more susceptible to military conflicts.

Prime Minister Abe's conservative Liberal Democratic Party (LDP)-led government returned to power in 2012. Since then, it has incrementally shifted Japan's defense posture to be able to deploy the country's potentially powerful Self-Defense Forces (SDF) more widely within the limits of the force-restricting Article 9. Recent nuclear adventurism of North Korea provided perfect pretext for a more active role of SDF in closer cooperation with the US forces. Should North Korea continue its series of ballistic missile tests, Japanese politicians in power would embark on a more determined path toward constitutional change.

Abe sets eyes on 2020 as time for action. National referendum is necessary. Perhaps the D-day would be set after the Tokyo Olympics in 2020, in the peak of Japanese nationalism. Abe's rhetoric is that Japan will "be born anew" as a normal country. Can he stay in power until then? Abe got reelected in 2017 for an unprecedented third three-year term. Abe became Japan's longest-serving post-war prime minister.

Whereas Japan is turning towards right-wing nationalism, its economic policy has turned towards globalism. Abenomics would not be complete without its structural reform to find a new engine for sustainable growth. After two decades of enclave in the seismic change of the ICT revolution, Japan embraced once again its second grand opening. The power elites in Tokyo aligned Japan's structural reform with its entry to TPP and strengthening the Japan-US alliance, as a key strategy to stand up to the threat from Beijing. The resurrection of the TPP in the name of CPTPP is a glaring signal that Japan has returned to the race. In Northeast Asia, in the era of the New Normal, where the US receded from its "Rebalancing to Asia" to "Make America Great Again," Japan emerged as a new guardian of free and open trade.

Korea under the wave of Populism

In the era of the New Normal, it is populism at the driver's seat of Korean politics. Korea, a global top 7 trading economy, proved extremely vulnerable to external shocks. The 2008 global economic crisis sent the country to another economic crisis. Thanks to its crisis management experience of dealing with the 1997 Asian financial crisis and structural reforms, Korea could get out of the troubles earlier than gloomy projections. Nonetheless, the crisis laid bare the limits of the Korean model.

Exposure to a couple of mega economic crises made clear that Korea's follower model ran its course. In the past, trade-oriented development strategy of Korea successfully elevated the living standards of Korean people to the ranks of advanced nation. Condensed growth gave rise to a group of high-flying global companies. The recipe for success was a combination of manufacturing, big business, and international trade. In the early days, the government played a decisive role in the allocation of scarce financial capital and the provision of incentives and penalties. Continued growth of Korean big business and their success in the global market changed the government-business relationship.

The democratization movement in the late 1980s sent the authoritarian regime to the history museum. Since 1987, Korea has become a liberal democracy. The political leader of the country was elected by the Korean people through free election. Contest has always been fierce among political parties. Election, not military coup nor revolution, has become the mechanism for power transition. Election in a liberal democracy is inherently based on populism. In a mature democracy, excessive electoral populism tends to get moderated through checks and balances mechanism built in the institution - free and critical media, market for ideas, legal system, and so on. In case of Korea, democratization after decades of political repression under authoritarian regime opened the flood gate of populism. Even after 30 years of democratization, Korean politics is yet to be mature. Political process is believed to mediate conflict and iron out differences through compromise. Korean politics has evolved toward an opposite path. Instead of reducing tensions, it has shown its competitiveness in escalating tension. Hence, surge of populism is the defining feature of the Korean political economy in the 21st century.

Surge of populism has seismic consequences in paradigm and policy making. Under the existential threat of losing power, Korea's right-wing party turned its ideological spectrum to more distribution and shared growth. Right-wing politicians stopped talking about economic growth, and started to learn the language of left-wing politicians. In their anticipation of preemption, they promised free school meals, reduced tuition fees, free health care, and free child care without any deep implications of fiscal burden. In fast-moving politics, measured approach to issues had no place. In the name of people, rosy promises were made.

Distributive politics has taken the driver's seat. Workers under aggressive labor unions demanded job stability and more slices of the pie for their share.

Implicit compromise during the condensed growth was that the government would allocate scarce financial capital to big firms, and the firms would create many stable jobs for workers. As long as the Korean economy was in the fast lane of high growth, the Korean social contract generated handsome profits, rising wages, a lot of stable jobs, growing brand value, national prestige, and elevated national pride.

Coming into the 21st century and going through a series of mega crisis – the 1997 econoic crisis and the 2008 global financial crisis, it became evident that a new social contract was in need. Disparities between the high-flying sector and the stagnant sector grew, with the negative consequences for the less-powerful and the less-mobile stakeholders. Tension between the government and the Chaebol (big business under the family control) got intensified. The government still had much power, particular in the regulations of business. The Chaebol has gone global. The government drew their political power from the local citizens, while the Chaebol drew their economic power from the global consumers.

With global reach, the Chaebol has outgrown the geopolitical territory of Korea. The fierce global competition forces them to be flexible and productive to stay competitive. The truth was they could not deliver a lot of stable jobs unlike good old days. Labor-intensive manufacturing had moved to China a long time ago. Korean big firms drew their source of profits from heavy and chemical industries, which are capital-intensive but labor-saving. Moreover, synchronization of the Korean business cycle along with the global economy increased business risk of being rigid. Increasing investment has not accompanied the creation of a lot of stable jobs, but only some jobs subject to the market fluctuation. The term "Jobless growth" became a frequent usage. Jobless growth was an exaggeration, but the nuance carried a grain of truth.

While disparities between the Chaebol and SMEs were growing, the Chaebol's reckless expansion into areas of small businesses, such as bakery, café, food, and grocery, raised eyebrows. Some Chaebols engaged in various anti-competitive internal transactions in their attempt to increase ownership of the largest shareholder and his family. Such mindless expansions met public back lash. The sense of noblesse oblige was not in the mindset of the growing Chabols. In a sense, they breached implicit contract by practicing monopolizing business behaviors in a small local market. Growing dominance of Chaebols on the basis of these anti-competitive and reckless moves irked the ire of the public. The Chaebols themselves volunteered to become a subject of reform. Demand for Chaebol reform was given an interesting name of "Economic Democratization." In fact, the term is originated from the Korean constitution of 1987, which was the outcome of political democratization - direct election of the President by the Korean people. In a political contest, one person exercises one vote. In an economic contest, one dollar carries one vote. The slogan of economic democratization intended to break the money power-based control of economic power. In the Presidential election of 2012, the right-wing incumbent party preemptively pledged to implement economic democratization. Hence, voters could not find any meaningful differences between the right-wing incumbent and the left-wing opponent when it came to the economic platform.

If truth be told, transformation of the Korean catch-up model to an innovation model was most urgent. Clouds of protracted growth slowdown, jobless growth, growing income disparities, and rapid aging were all interconnected phenomena. Reform of Chaebols and the labor sector demanded immediate attention. The Korean model of welfare society should be invented. One critical question remained. Where to find new sources of sustainable growth? Seeking the new blueprint of economic growth was the utmost priority. All reform tasks need to be aligned with this new vision.

The consensus among policy experts was to embark on "Service Big Bang."[76] The idea behind this was that service sector has the largest employment status (about 70% of total jobs), but the Korean service sector lagged behind other countries in terms of productivity and scale. Without fundamentally revamping the moribund service sector, the future of the Korean economy would be the same as the Lost Decades of Japan, or even worse. The vision of the Service Big Bang was to turn this miserable state of the Korean service sector into an opportunity. Myriads of hurdles stand in the way. The most visible barriers were the regulatory burden and red tapes, which date back to the early days of economic take off, but failed to keep up with the times.

76 For the fuller account of "Service Big Bang", refer to Choi (2014).

The right-wing government of Korea of Lee Myung-bak and Park Geun-hye failed to champion the vision of Service Big Bang and vigorously implement it. They could not set the vision straight. The vision was not clear enough, sending incoherent and noisy signals to stakeholders. Slogans without clear vision is what rhetoric is all about. In retrospect, inability and incompetence of the right-wing regime not setting the vision of the Service Big Bang, and not undertaking Chaebol reform and labor reform is just remarkable. After all, they are all right-wing agenda. They got the chance in the critical moment, but let opportunities slip through their fingers.

Now, the newly elected government of President Moon Jae-in, which came to power in the aftermath of the impeachment of former President Park, turned to the far-left. The government of Moon set the slogan of income-led growth. The policy inscription has a long list, including increasing minimum wage through a series of high jumps, turning irregular workers into regular workers, reducing long-work hours, increasing government sector jobs, and so on.

Without doubt, what they pursue is a typical income redistribution policy. The motivation is to provide more income to the lower-income group so that they can spend more. The proponents of the so-called income-led growth argue for the virtuous circle of "increased consumption ▶ increased sale ▶ increased jobs ▶ further increased incomes ▶ further increased consumption." They base their logic on the higher consumption propensity for lower income groups. The income-led growth has been under attack. The most potent attack is that income is not a source of growth, but an outcome of growth. Even the neutral side argues that although income redistribution would be necessary for social cohesion and to narrow down the disparities, income redistribution policy is not a sustainable growth strategy at all.

President Moon is avowedly pro-labor and pursues the policy of strengthening protection of workers. Between jobs and workers, though, it is not clear which gets protected. Consensus among experts is that it is workers, not jobs, which should be protected. Politicians seem clueless, though. Protecting workers would require training and upgrading skill. Effects of this policy is not immediate. Protecting jobs, on the other hand, would generate more immediate and visible effect, even though it may prove eventually unsustainable. Myopic bureaucratic interests and short-term political gain would favor the unsustainable protection of jobs. This means heightened obstacles for the navigation of the Korean economy.

The Korean conundrum

It has been some time since Korean economic growth has been underperforming compared to world economic growth, showing premature slow-down. Korea, once a proud champion of globalism, has lost its growth dynamism. Whether right-wing or left-wing, politics leaned far towards populism. At the average per capita income of US $ 30,000 - the average of OECD member countries, the sense of complacency is wide spread. Demand for redistributive politics does not show signs of abating. Considering silver tsunami, and dimmed prospects for the lower income group, demand for redistributive politics will be all the more in the rise.

Transferring income from high to low without generating new source of growth would not be sustainable at all. Nonetheless, the short-sighted nature of Korean politics is making Korea just stay on the course, without daring to seek other trajectories. Korea has already spent a "Lost Decade", failing to find a new pathway. It did not make a determined investment in search of a new growth formula. It did not bother to generate the sense of urgency for paradigm shift among the people. Politics have been reactionary, opportunistic, and partisan. The past successful strategy of turning the external forces of globalization into a momentum for domestic reform and innovation is increasingly rare in Korea. Globalism is under attack. In Korea, perhaps like in many other corners in the world, globalism is labeled as neo-liberalism, which is blamed for causing much pain to the economic minority - farmers, workers, small business, and the young generation - and also causing economic dislocation and chaos.

In Northeast Asia, Korea has the highest trade dependency ratio (Figure 9).[77] As of 2016, Korea's trade dependency ratio is about 80%, having peaked to the level of 110% in the early 2010s. China's trade dependency ratio has steadily increased and it peaked to above 60% in time period 2005-2006. Recently, it has shown gradual declining. As of 2016, China's trade dependency ratio is about 40%. Trade dependency ratio of Japan had been

77 Trade dependency ratio of a country is measured by the share of trade of the country out of its GDP.

stable around 20% level until the early years of the 21st century. Since the 2008 global crisis Japan's trade dependency ratio has shown a gradual increase.

Compared to China and Japan, Korea's trade dependency ratio is quite high. High-trade dependency means high sensitivity to external factors. The rising tide of protectionism throws Korea into more daunting challenges than other countries in Northeast Asia. The emergence of New Normal implies that Korea has the largest stake in the deep institutionalization of Northeast Asia. Considering the surge of populism in Korea, such a move towards deep institutionalization should be inclusive, ensuring the disadvantageous and less powerful players not falling behind.

Figure 9. Trade dependency ratio of Northeast Asia countries

(unit: %)

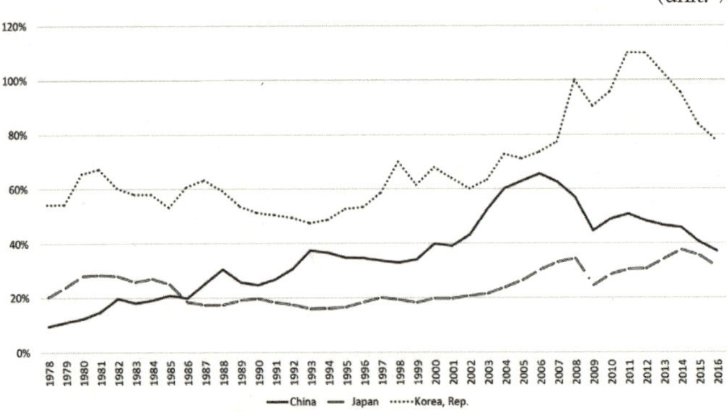

**Source: World Bank

In the domestic arena, populism has advanced in China and Korea, while right-wing nationalism is gaining momentum in Japan. In foreign relations, nationalism has taken over China, pushing globalism away. Korea has also distanced from globalism and inched toward nationalism. Interestingly, Japan turned to globalism. Newly emerging ideological landscape reveals difficulties ahead for deep institutionalization. Important implication is that the future path of deep institutionalization should be aligned with "Inclusive Growth", caring more about the losers from competition.[78]

3. Northeast Asia and the US: Into Uncharted Territory

The postwar international order in Northeast Asia would not have shaped and evolved into the current form without US involvement and planning. Democratic Japan under the market economy is the architect of the US, which came to rule the defeated Japan. The US, along with the UN forces and Korean soldiers, fought in the Korea war. The US military alliance with Korea and Japan provided each country the essential security protection for economic growth. The US engagement policy of China since the early 1970s laid important foundations for peace and prosperity in Northeast Asia. The cooperative era of the US-China relations has passed

78 Acemoglu and Robinson (2012) argue that the growth generated by extractive institutions is not sustainable. From their perspective, China's growth would come to an end, unless China makes transition to inclusive institution.

away. In its place, the new normal of confrontation and containment is surfacing.

US-China Relations: From Engagement to Confrontation

Broken Fantasy

Even prior to the 2016 presidential election of Donald Trump, whose China bashing has defined his campaign, policy makers and experts of Washington had converged in reckoning that the United States' approach to China has failed. What has driven the US approach to China since Nixon's historic trip to Beijing in 1972, which melted the ice between the US and China, and set the course for China's return to the global stage, was the assumption that deepening ties would transform China towards a political economic system, with a more open market and more political freedom. After almost half a century of engagement with China, it is increasingly clear that the record so far does not measure up to the assumption. Moreover, the future course of China is less likely to be converging on such a desirable course, as previously imagined by US policy makers.

Washington power elites have been debating what went wrong, and trying to come up with a more realistic workable approach. **What went wrong?** Did the US put too much faith in its power to shape China's trajectory? In retrospect, the US was too complacent due to its triumph of the Cold War and believed that the time was with its side. Such complacency possibly led the US to underestimate the ambition and strategic cunningness of China. From the strategic view point of China, it played "defensive" well to earn time before it built sufficient capacity. The US strategy of engaging with China gave birth to Chinese membership at the WTO. Coming into the 21st century, China kept rising under the Factory China in full swing. In the early new millennium, the US did not take the Chinese challenge seriously. The prevailing mood in Washington was that China will be a responsible stakeholder in the US-led global system. "Peaceful rise" of China, a term coined by Beijing, found a powerful group of cheerleaders in Washington. Surely, there were some critical of Beijing, warning its insidious ambition.

The adopted approach in Washington was to treat China as a responsible partner, not simply because the US really believed that China would behave as such, but more because China would not deviate much from the comfort zone of the existing global system under such treatment.[79] But for this line of thinking, it would be hard to understand the US unwillingness to confront China's well-documented practices of currency manipulation. The US-China relationship has been characterized by strategic cooperation until the onset of the second decade of this new century. From Washington's point of view, they exerted extreme care not to confront and provoke China in their calculation not to isolate the reform-minded in Beijing. The lure of

79 The thinking at the time is aptly explained by Joseph Nye: "If we treated China as an enemy, we were guaranteeing an enemy in the future. If we treated China as a friend, we could not guarantee friendship, but we could at least keep open the possibility of more benign outcomes." Requoted from Campbell (2018).

the growing Chinese market for the US business sector added more sweeteners. Hence, the engagement has been the prevailing coalition in Washington for a quite long time.

It takes two to tango. Maintaining cooperation between the reigning superpower and the rising power with hegemonic ambition also finds two strange bedfellows. Beijing made extensive care not to break such hopeful thinking of Washington. Even as China moved to strengthen and modernize its military power on the basis of its newfound wealth, China managed to put the US at ease. Case in point is Beijing's reaction to the jargon of G-2, which enjoyed large circulation in the global community. The term G-2 was coin by Fred Bergsten in 2008.[80] The idea was to bring China on board to assume a role of significant partnership in resolving the global problem of economic crisis, global imbalance, stalled trade talks, and global warming.

As the leading country of emerging-market economies and the world's largest surplus/creditor country, China was pressed hard to play a role of G-2, not just a passive member of the global economic system. Beijing's response was lukewarm at best. The official response of China was that it was not ready to assume such a great role, because China was still a developing country with so many urgent domestic agenda to be taken care of. Beijing thought it was premature to play its grown role under the limelight. Still they played the game pursuant to the playbook of Deng, who advised a cautious,

80. Bergsten (2008)

moderate foreign policy path for a century. Such a low-profile posture of Beijing made Washington less alarmed.

However, it did not take much time for Beijing to change its foreign policy stance. Around the time of leadership transfer to Xi in 2012, China turned around and discarded its long-held strategy of "hide your brightness and bid your time." Until then, Beijing had effectively managed to be big and competitive without being confrontational. Now, Washington is busy with the belated post mortem of its failed policy toward China. The testimony of Kurt Campbell serves an illustration, who served as the Assistant Secretary of the State Department for East Asian and Pacific Affairs (2009-2013):

> "*All sides of the policy debate erred: free traders and financiers who foresaw inevitable and increasing openness in China, integrationists who argued that Beijing's ambitions would be tamed by greater interaction with the international community, and hawks who believed that China's power would be abated by perpetual American primacy. Neither carrots nor sticks have swayed China as predicted. Diplomatic and commercial engagement have not brought political and economic openness. Neither U.S. military power nor regional balancing has stopped Beijing from seeking to displace core components of the U.S.-led system. And the liberal international order has failed to lure or bind China as powerfully as expected. China has instead pursued its own course, belying a range of American expectations in the process.*"[81]

81 Campbell (2018). Lee Kuan Yew observed: "China is not going to become a liberal

In August 2017 Cambridge University Press confirmed it had removed access to more than 300 articles from readers in China following pressure from the Chinese government. Cambridge University Press stated they blocked this material in China to avoid having their entire publication blocked. The press published a list of the articles removed, which included sensitive topics such as the Tiananmen protest of 1989, Pro-democracy movements in Hong Kong, and the negative effects of the Cultural Revolution. The academic community criticized the decision of Cambridge University Press to self-censor. The Western press reported that this fiasco was a part of intensified crack-down on diversity since Xi Jinping took power.

China now is not the China as in the US playbook any more. China is no longer a rising power. China is a risen power with its sphere of influence not confined to the region of East Asia. China is not keeping a low profile any longer. It flexes its muscle in various places in the world. China has been intensifying its influence campaign in the world. Not being content with cyber censorship inside of China, China has mounted its pressure on foreign countries with the aim of purging "forbidden words" from circulation. The

---

democracy: if it did, it would collapse···. To achieve the modernization of China, her Communist leaders are prepared to try all and every method, except for democracy with one person and one vote in a multi-party system." (Quoted from Alison and Blackwill 2013)

list of forbidden words from Beijing include Tiananmen, Taiwan, Tibet, Dalai Lama, Xinjiang, and so on. Troubling signs are everywhere and growing in numbers.

The summer of 2017 witnessed the beleaguered Cambridg University Press between pressure from Beijing to delete forbidden words from the search menu and protest by scholars not to succumb to such unprecedented demand. The Cambridge University Press agreed to the censorship of China Quarterly, a renowned academic journal for China, removing 315 articles.[82] Only after vehement protest from the academic circle, the press reinstated them.

In the same summer, several university professors in the Western world faced angry protests from Chinese students. In August 2017, the professor at the University of Newcastle, who had referred to Taiwan as an independent country, faced angry protest from a Chinese student in the class. Chinese students released footage online - filmed secretly in classes - of the incident. Eventually, the university had to face the complaint of the Chinese consulate.[83] This episode is one of many and rising tension between foreign academics and China. In June 2017, University of Sydney was demanded by the Chinese consulate to reconsider holding a forum on the Tiananmen Square protests of 1989.

These incidents shows China's increasingly bold influence campaign

82 Huang and (2017)

83 Riordan and Callick (2017)

targeting the Western academics, which coined the term of "sharp power of China"[84] The Western world is taking the sharp power of China seriously. For instance, in March 2018, the Defense Department of Australia prohibited WeChat, a social text message service originated from China, for security concern.[85] This move followed the decision by the US military ban of the Chinese-made drones few months ago.

Confucius Institutes (孔子学院), which have been set up in foreign countries for the purpose of public education by the Chinese government, have been on the subject of suspicion of challenging resources from Beijing for this ideological influence campaign. In the US Congress, a bill is being draft to require Confucius Institutes to register as foreign agents.

China is not passively accepting the global rule. It attempts to create a new rule book. Belt Road Initiative is China's multi-dimensional global influence campaign. China aims to bring the entire region along the passage of Belt and Road in the shadow of its influence. Beijing successfully launched the AIIB against all odds. All in all, China is not playing the game as set by the US. The US has lost some early battles. These new developments are not something Washington is prepared to accept.

When did China change its strategy? What propelled China to throw its veil of hiding and waiting and choose to be daring and confrontational?

84 Walker and Ludwig (2017)

85 Chen and Deng(2018)

China's growing confidence drew from China's strengthened economic power, the decline of the US, and dysfunctional Western systems. Multiple and simultaneous development of these events rendered the Chinese power elites to reconsider its global strategy. After internal debate, China came to the conviction that its time has arrived, and decided to play more aggressively and assertively. "The New Type of the Great Power Relations" is Beijing's answer to the US call for the G-2. In the first summit between Obama and Xi, Xi is allegedly said to Obama, "The vast Pacific Ocean has enough space for two great powers." Xi's remarks intended to challenge Obama's Rebalancing to Asia strategy.

The second decade of the 21st century will be recorded in the emergence of the New Normal in the US-China relations. Obama had changed the US approach to China to containment and confrontation from the conventional approach of strategic partnership. Surely, it did not give up the frame of strategic partnership altogether. For instance, in the area of climate change, Obama worked hard to get the collaboration and concession from China, the world's biggest polluter. In the area of trade and security, Rebalancing to Asia was the newly adopted grand strategy. Under this strategic scheme, the US championed the TPP and tried to block China's initiative to create the AIIB.

Now what? With the election of President Trump, the new US approach toward China appears to be more and more confrontational. The US and China are in a collision course. The question is when, not whether. At the present, Trump needs assistance from Beijing in mounting maximum pressure on North Korea to deal with the increasing likelihood of exposing the US under the threat of nuclear weapons.

To many, the Trump administration's stubborn adherence to reciprocity and bilateralism evades logic and common sense. Trump's decision to withdraw the US from the TPP caught them off guard. The TPP was, to many experts, probably a most effective strategy to contain China. Trump should have run with the TPP all the way, if he were true to his criticism that China is an unfair and unruly cheater.[86] Still many is hopeful that the US would return to the TPP sooner, not later, even under the Trump administration.

By all means, China is determined to be on the path to becoming a military power with the capability of global projection. China is not the same as the Soviet Union, which was strong in technology but failed in its commercialization. The US grand strategy of containing the Soviet Union and blocking commercialization attempt played a critical role in the demise of the Soviet Union. China is different. Perhaps, the US confronts the most dynamic and formidable competitor in modern history.

China's place in the globe is mainly due to its commercial success, riding high the wave of globalization, and intensifying global linkage. Swimming the turbulent sea of globalization, China learned how to play with the world and became a master of the game. The New China is a powerful, ambitious,

86 The sense of frustration was manifest in the words of Thomas Friedman, a New York Times columnist. He ran his opinion with the title of "Trump is a Chinese agent." (Friedman 2017).

determined, yet pragmatic if necessary, and so delicately interwoven with the outside world. Socialism with Chinese characteristics has a bizarre combination of a strong state and the market. Its remarkable success gave rise to the so-called state capitalism. A popular commentary is that the 21st century will see the contest between state capitalism and market capitalism. Such a frame fails to note a critical point. What is happening in China is not state capitalism, but state monopoly. The state, which is identical to the Chinese Communist Party, controls the entire spectrum of the economic system. Even the dazzling success of the mobile economy is only due to the protection of domestic industries and the blocking of foreign entry. China came to possess unparalleled hard power and "sharp power" with global reach. How far can it go?

4. External Risk: Silver Tsunami, Race against the Machine

The Northeast Asia region, a major manufacturing power house of the world, is facing gigantic external risk: "Silver Tsunami" (Rapid Aging) and "Race against the Machine" (Digital Transformation).[87] Unparalleled speed

87 Race Against the Machine is in fact the title of the book by Brynjolfsson and McAfee (2011). Their book has subtitle, "How the Digital Revolution is Accelerating Innovation, Driving Productivity, and Irreversibly Transforming Employment and the Economy", which captures the essence of challenges confronted by Northeast Asian manufacturing-centered economy.

of aging has already swallowed Japan. The speed of aging is measured by the timing of a society entering an "aging society" (more than 7% of the population with age of 65 years and over) to an "aged society" (more than 14% of the population with age of 65 years and over), and then to an "hyper-aged society" (more than 20% of the population with age of 65 years and over). Having entered the aging society in 2000, Korea entered the aging society in 2017. Korea has taken 17 years from entering the aging society to the aged society. The projection is that Korea will enter the stage of hyper-aged society in 2026. This speed of aging is a world-record setting pace. The previous record was set by Japan. Japan took 35 years from entering an aging society (1970) to a hyper-aged society (2005). Silver tsunami is also about to overtake China soon. China moved to an aging society in 2001, and is projected to enter a hyper-aged society in 2035. Due to its population size and speedy aging, China is now the only country in the world with more than 100 million people of 65 years-old and older.

Improvement of living standards, access to health care, and advance in medical science have contributed to higher longevity for the people in Northeast Asia. Low birth rate coupled with increased longevity gave rise to the Silver tsunami, an unprecedented speed of aging. The asymmetry between aging population and social safety net for the elderly is a grave source for concern and worry. Japan has not built a rather solid welfare society. As a matter of fact, the "Lost Decades" of Japan is ascribed to its speedy aging in the midst of a weak social safety net. The retired elderly, without a stable steady income generation, and also with weak social safety net, decided to spend less and save more for a long and cold winter of their life. (The Japanese have the highest longevity in the world.) The huge mismatch between increased production capacity and dampened aggregate consumption is blamed for the "Lost Decades" of Japan. Situations in Korea and China may be even worse. Elderly poverty rate for Korea is the worst among OECD nations. Although no comparable data exists for China, which is not member of the OECD, poverty of the elderly poverty, as documented by some internal Chinese sources, is allegedly miserable.

The Silver Tsunami heralds the end of labor-intensive manufacturing, the end of unskilled works, and demands for a solid welfare state. The very nature of growth needs to be transformed. Growth policy favoring the top 1 percent will find less political and intellectual support in the age of jobless growth and lessened trickle-down effect. Income redistribution to the less powerful from the powerful will not work, either. Without continuous growth, it would end as just a one-time political event. Overcoming the Silver Tsunami requires a paradigm shift to inclusive growth, which helps ensure shared benefits among all stakeholders so that "growth lifts all boats," not "growth lifts only yachts."

The risk of Silver Tsunami comes to the shore with a new technological revolution - the 4th Industrial Revolution. For the Northeast Asia region, the Digital Tsunami presents an existential threat. Through connecting and combining offline and online, key enabling technologies of the 4th Industrial Revolution - Drone, 3D printer, AI, Internet of Things (IOT), Big data, Smart Factory, robots - are producing new ways of organizing economic and social activities. A number of reports compete to foretell the brave future. Low-skilled jobs and routine activities are already replaced by robots and AIs. The future of business seems driven by imagination, not by perspiration. Amazon, which started its business in on-line book delivery, has replaced offline book stores. Market value of Uber, taxi-riding service start-up, which has no assembly line for auto production, was once assessed to be higher than that of GM, one of the largest auto companies in the worl d.[88] The Digital Tsunami threatens to upend the brick and mortar industry of Northeast Asia.

5. Case for Coordinated Inclusive Growth

Turning Risk into Opportunities

The twin mega external risks have silver linings. As the Chinese character of risk illustrates, risk has two faces: threat and opportunity. Perception and strategic approach could turn threat into an opportunity. The Silver Tsunami and the Digital Tsunami, taken together, may offer a new business horizon for an economy in general, and the elderly and the economic minority in particular.

88 Forbes (2015) reported that "At $68 billion valuation, market value of Uber is bigger than that of GM, Ford, and Honda". The valuation of the start-up, of which shares are not traded in the stock market, cannot be precise. Moreover, there is a tendency for overvaluing companies in new technology sector. In late 2017, Uber was valued at about $48 billion, according to Forbes (2018).

Unparalleled speed of aging, combined with disruptive digital revolution, threatened the likelihood of increasing disparities in the future of Northeast Asia. If not checked, business as usual would worsen, not lessen, distributional consequences of growth. A society may lose cohesiveness along the lines of age divide and digital divide. Prolonged such divides would provide fertile grounds for magnifying unreasonable populism and unhealthy nationalism. More and more, reform-minded globalists would find less and less room to stand. Hence, the case for inclusive growth becomes imperative.

The vison of inclusive growth is to have the rising tide lift all boats, not just few luxurious yachts. To set a clear vision to guide inclusive growth, paradigm shift should be implemented. Northeast Asia's strategy to overcome the Silver Tsunami and the Digital Tsunami should be effectively linked to its vision of paradigm shift. Shift from manufacturing-driven to innovation-driven is imperative. In this historic paradigm shift for inclusive growth, three fronts of battle zone deserve emphasizing.

a. contest between pro-deepening versus pro-status quo.

b. going-it-alone national strategy versus coordinated global strategy

c. Priority between manufacturing versus service sector

1. Pro-Deepening Coalition

In each Northeast Asia state, a contest is going on between pro-deepening coalition and pro-status-quo coalition. "Pro-deepening" group seeks more integration of their country with the global economy. They speak for increased trade and investment, and argue for dismantling barriers which stand in the way for enhanced link with the global economy. Status-quo coalition is in the opposite of the ideological spectrum.

Global business and liberal intellectual lead the pro-deepening coalition. Import-competing sectors, labor groups and non-governmental groups in the name of sovereignty are main components of the status-quo coalition. The contest has been always very tense and tight. During the days of economic take-off and catch-up, pro-deepening coalition has outnumbered. With the end of catch up in sight, and with the emergence of the New Normal, pro-deepening coalition is being outnumbered by status-quo coalition.

Visionary leadership may play a role of game changer in this political setting. In retrospect, the Northeast Asia region had faced some moments of truth and rose to the occasion. China's pursuit to join the WTO (1986-2001), Korea's drive for the KORUS FTA (2006-2011), and Japan's decision to join the TPP (2012) were defining moments. Daring to look to the visionary yet uncertain future was doubtlessly risky political action. However, political leadership was above short-term calculations. They fought against the temptation of no action, vigilantly communicated with the opposed, and measured up to the challenges.

On the other hand, the region has its moments of indecisiveness. Korea's refusal to complete BIT negotiations with the US (2002), Japan's hesitance in matching Korea's aggressive posture in the Korea-Japan FTA negotiations (2004), and China's lack of implementing its ambitious reform blueprint of

2013 are in the list.

What divides the former category and the latter category is the difference between leadership. In both cases, the domestic political landscape was more or less identical. Balance between pro-deep coalition and pro-status-quo was very tight. Determined leadership of pro-active strategic pursuit of long-term national interest gave rise to the outcome in the first category. Reactionary leadership of inaction and indecisiveness torn between pros and cons, captured by power base, led to the outcome in the second category.

2. Coordinated Approach Imperative

Going-it-alone strategy will likely to be short-sighted at the expense of long-term efficiency for everyone involved. China's industrial policy at its powerful display in Made in China 2025 is a case in point. China may succeed in building its capacity by limiting foreign access to its market. The sheer size of its domestic market, one of the largest in the world and, perhaps, being on the way to overtake the US to become number one, may offer a reason for China's confidence. In fact, however, realities may be the opposite. Chinese policy makers need to turn their eyes to the case of Japan in the 1990s.

In the 1990s, the wave of ICT revolution was sweeping the world. Various new technologies were born and contested their way to market. Japan was an obvious target. Upon the surge of ICT, Japan decided to pursue a strategy of isolation. It was a puzzling move, considering Japan's solid electronics industry. Instead of opening up their market and riding the wave of ICT, Japanese policy makers thought they should defend their market from foreign access. To them, the size of the Japanese market, the second largest in the world, and about to overtake the US to become number one, was their source for confidence.

Consequences of such a policy decision are for all eyes to see. Korea took advantage of Japan's inward-looking strategy. Korean industries and companies, which were all out to catch up Japanese ones, forged ahead, while Japan got stuck. Korea's structural reform and market opening paved the way for the rise of "ICT power Korea" in the global stage. Korea leap-frogged Japan in ICT.

3. Vision of Service Big Bang

A paradigm shift to innovation-driven economy in Northeast Asia is a compelling yet belated call for placing priority on the service sector. So far, the service sector in Northeast Asia remained as untapped potential. No mature industrial economy has ever enjoyed the situation where the manufacturing industry contributes more jobs than the service sector. Without any solid scientific logic behind such a stylized pattern, rough estimates for the maximum share of job from the manufacturing sector was 30 percent. This number is from the peak time of Germany in its relentless pursuit of industrialization. China had more share from manufacturing, as a rapid developing economy. The majority of jobs are from the service sector.

Compared to a mature economy, the service sector of Northeast Asia is in a sorry state. It is remarkably unproductive, inefficient, and fragmented.

Low productivity in the service sector spells for low wage. Low wage means long working hours without upgrading skills and reforming supporting institutional structures. This leads to low productivity being sustained. Hence, there is a vicious circle. In this sense, the service sector in Northeast Asia gets trapped.

The mindset of politicians and policymakers makes the situation worse. To their minds, services are not something to be provided through the market. This prehistoric mindset is in sharp contrast with their mindsets for manufactured products. While a number of promotional policies were invented and relentlessly pursed in the manufacturing sector, the story in the service sector was filled with stifling regulation, red tapes, ring of corruption, prevalence of incumbents through generations, blocking new entry, and so on. The biggest victim was the consumers, who were underserved. Time has finally arrived to rectify this asymmetry.

7 Looking to the Future:
Trajectories to Northeast Asia 2030

1. Competing Approaches for Deep Institutionalization

Considering the sustainable economic growth and political stability in the region, the most desirable course of action is to agree on a trilateral FTA, which is comprehensive in terms of coverage and advanced in terms of commitment. Such an agreement seems evasive and out of reach. Hence, Korea, Japan, and China, reflecting their own preference in agenda and level of commitment, have been pursuing a Plan B strategy. Agenda means the menu for negotiations from goods, services, investment, and rules on Old Economy and New Economy.[89] Commitment means market opening

89 Old Economy and New Economy are used for the purpose of comparison between the conventional economic activities and the newly emerging economy, driven by the digital revolution (so-called the 4th industrial revolution). Often, the terms of 20th century economy and the 21st century economy are used in the public discourse to mean Old Economy and New Economy. These terms are in the circulation to provoke policy debate, not meant to be rigorous.

promise. Three approaches are in play now. Each approach is motivated by strategic preemption to gain negotiation leverage at the China-Japan-Korea trilateral level of the deep institutionalization race.

First, Bottom-up approach

In this approach, countries try to negotiate bilateral trade agreements in their hope to create a strong basis for a trilateral trade agreement. In the case of NAFTA, the presence of the US-Canada FTA played a key building block. In the case of EU, a solid Franco-German alliance was instrumental. In Northeast Asia, at the present there is only one bilateral FTA, one between Korea and China. The Korea-Japan FTA negotiations have been long suspended since 2004, while there is no attempt to launch the Japan-China FTA.

Second, Top-down approach

In this approach, countries engage in regional and mega-regional trade agreements with anticipation that it would create a basis for a trilateral trade agreement. TPP 11 and RCEP compete are vying each other in this approach. As of March 2018, TPP 11 becomes a reality in the name of CPTPP. RCEP is still being negotiated with a goal of concluding by the end of 2018. In fact, the deadline has been a moving target for some time. At the present, neither China nor ASEAN seems in charge of the negotiations, while the offers from India are regarded as unconstructive to move the talks forward.

Third, Out-to-In approach

In this approach, countries in Northeast Asia attempt to establish trade agreements with major non-regional countries (in our analysis, the US and EU) with a view to create an edge in the next stage of deep institutionalization race in Northeast Asia. Korea's bilateral FTA with the US and with the EU provoked competition in the region. Japan followed with the TPP, in essence the Japan-US FTA, and also with an FTA with the EU. China is far behind in the race. China has no FTA negotiations with either the US or EU. China's on-going BIT talks may serve its launching pad for the next level of the game.

2. Trajectories to 2030: Analysis

Bottom-up

The Bottom-up approach is unlikely to be effective. The one and only bilateral FTA in Northeast Asia, the Korea-China FTA, falls short in terms of agenda and commitment to be qualified as an effective platform for deep institutionalization in the region. The Korea-China FTA, as concluded in December 2014 and became effective from December 2015, achieved only 90% of tariff elimination, compared to 98% of the Korea-US FTA and 99% of the Korea-EU FTA. More significantly, it fails to include liberalization commitments and rule-making in service and investment. As a built-in agenda, negotiations on service and investment have been postponed to the second stage, of which talks would commence from 2018. The fate of these talks is tightly tied to the Chinese government's willingness to reform and open its service sector and investment regime. Notwithstanding President Xi's repeated rhetoric, China does not have a comprehensive plan for opening up service and investment, except for the current experiments with Free Trade Zones (FTZ). Even FTZs have been undertaken as a pilot showcase with a slow-paced gradualism without a strong passion.

If bottom-up approach is to be a viable path toward deep institutionalization in the region, the Korea-Japan FTA with comprehensive coverage and high-level commitment should be attempted. The talks were attempted in 2003, only to be suspended a year later. Back then, the Korean government insisted on more liberalization commitment in the Japanese agricultural sector, and on negotiations on NTM. The Japanese government could not accept any of these two requests. Now, the situation has changed. The Japanese government can address these two agenda, as evidenced by its negotiations with the US for the TPP, and with the EU.

Suppose the Japanese government is more willing to negotiate these two issues as demanded by the Korean side. Then the ball will be in the court of Korea. Within Korea, there exists a strong import bias against Japanese products. In particular, Korean automobile-makers fear that Japanese automobiles would flood the Korean market while Korean companies could sell virtually none in the Japanese market. Foreign share in the Japanese automobile market is six percent - the lowest among OECD member states - and the share of Korean auto is virtually nil. In fact, the Korean auto market is already much open to the Japanese auto. Without effectively addressing this opposition from the local auto industry, the Korea-Japan FTA will not be able to move forward. The complicated diplomatic relationship between Korea and Japan would not be conducive to resume bilateral trade talks either.

Top-down

In terms of completeness, TPP 11 is ahead of the game. TPP 11 has resurrected from the breakdown of TPP. It will become an international treaty among 11 original members of the TPP, excluding the US. TPP 11 is given its official name of Comprehensive and Progressive Agreement for Trans-Pacific Partnership (CPTPP). CPTPP is expected to be effective in 2019, after getting ratification from its signatories. In essence CPTPP is the same as TPP. In the anticipation of the return of the US, about a dozen provisions in the TPP are reportedly suspended.

For CPTPP to be a catalyst in a Top-down approach for deep institutionalization in Northeast Asia, the participation of Korea and China should take place. In the light of the severe gap between commitments in CPTPP and the capacity and willingness of China, the Chinese membership in CPTPP is an unlikely scenario for the foreseeable future. Even if the Chinese government may possess its capacity to accept the CPTPP, China may not pursue to join for some political reason. Hence, the key is Korea. If Korea joins CPTPP, it will create interesting dynamics. With Japan and Korea in CPTPP, China will become isolated. In that scenario, the game is whether China would join CPTPP or not. However, Korea's membership in CPTPP is not something for sure. As analyzed before, Korea's membership in CPTPP will become only possible if and only if Korea and Japan negotiate successfully their mutual concerns.

RCEP is yet to reach its conclusion. Since its first negotiations in 2013, seventeen rounds of official negotiations have been conducted. If somehow RCEP becomes a reality, China, Japan, and Korea would have a sort-of trilateral agreement within the context of RCEP, which is composed of ASEAN and six non-ASEAN countries. Given the coverage of agenda and expected level of commitment, RCEP is not likely to emulate TPP 11, nor something equivalent to NAFTA or the EU. The implication is that a successful RCEP would provide a baseline for further negotiations among China, Japan, and Korea. The baseline will fall short on coverage, because the RCEP is, to a large extent, expected to be weak on New Economy. If RCEP gets completed without any meaningful rules on State Owned Enterprise (SOE), E-Commerce, Regulatory Coherence, Labor, and Environment, which are very much related to the Chinese economy, the next stage of negotiations for deep institutionalization among China, Japan, and Korea is promised to be a long and winding road.

Outside-In

The Outside-In approach has been, in fact, heavily used in opening up the closed domestic market of Japan, Korea, and China. Strong external market opening pressures from the US have played catalysts for opening up. The governments of those countries have turned external pressures to triggers for reform and opening. The 1980s - 1990s have plenty of these episodes. On the basis of fair and reciprocal market access, the US demanded Japan and Korea to open up the agriculture sector, the service sector (financial service and telecommunications as priorities), IPR, and so on. The Chinese government has also turned the WTO accession negotiations to an opportunity to open its closed market to the world.

As preemptive strategy to enhance negotiating leverage for the race to deepen institutionalization, Korea is ahead of game. Japan is making serious and steadfast effort to get even. Japan is about to complete an FTA negotiations with the EU. The only sticking point is investment protection. In December 2017, the two sides announced that they came to an agreement in all tariffs, non-tariffs, and rules-related agenda. The departure of the US from the TPP is a main source of incompletion in Japan's strategic map. Japan almost had an FTA with the US. With the completion of CPTPP, the choice of Japan is binary:

Either Japan strikes an FTA with the US one-on-one, or Japan manages to bring the US into CPTPP. The first option is doable if Japan becomes interested in the idea of a one-on-one. Shortly after Trump pulled the US out of the TPP, the US indicated its interest in a bilateral FTA with Japan. Back then, Japan was in shock of the unravelling of the TPP. Tokyo was fearful that a bilateral FTA with Washington would lead to more opening up, compared to the TPP. Now Tokyo has CPTPP under its arsenal. Note that Tokyo also reached an agreement with Washington in the context of the TPP. The current US government under President Trump would demand more opening from Tokyo, compared to the US-Japan agreement in TPP. All in all, Tokyo needs to embrace more opening-up, if it wishes to attract Washington to its game plan. Tokyo will carefully weigh the likelihood of each scenario, along with the associated political risks.

In the case of the US returning to CPTPP, of which prospect is highly speculative, Japan would have decisive edge in the second stage race. If such a scenario - the return of the US to CPTPP - becomes more than a hypothetical amusement, Korea will be forced to consider its accession to CPTPP seriously. As a matter of fact, negotiating with Japan under such a scenario would be more politically manageable to the Korean government, compared to one-on-one negotiations with Japan.

Prolonged delay of the US return to CPTPP, which is a safe bet for now, will make Tokyo entertain the other choice - the US-Japan FTA - more seriously. The decision will be closely related to threat from Beijing. If Tokyo becomes politically committed to the idea of a bilateral FTA with Washington, then the game will move forward. In case of successful negotiations on the US-Japan FTA, both Korea and Japan would have a bilateral FTA with the US and the EU, respectively. Interesting negotiating dynamics may unfold. Seoul and Tokyo may embark on a trilateral trade agreement by bringing the US on board.

Successful Outside-In approach would create an express way to the next race of deepening institutionalization. Under this scenario, both Korea and Japan are connected to the US and the EU in one way or another, whereas China would be isolated unless it accelerates its pace of reform and open.

3. China against the West: Standardization vs Harmonization

In the race for deepening institutionalization in Northeast Asia, the Chinese approach is radically different from the Western approach. The Western approach is best represented by standardization, a common platform under which countries are willing to bind their regulatory system. As analyzed before, the global flow in investment and service sectors has been largely outside of the WTO multilateral trading system. The DDA has been a gross failure to develop further disciplines on this urgent issue. The neck-breaking speed of ICT revolution and the arrival of the digital revolution, in which off-line and on-line are merged to reshape economic activities and give rise to new industries, have taken place irrespective of the global trading system. Different domestic regulatory regimes and practices would impede further growth potential, if these differences are not effectively coordinated.

Due to the polarized structure of the WTO between the Western economies and the developing ones, the US and the EU have been trying to develop trade rules outside of the WTO. TPP and TTIP (Transatlantic Trade and Investment Partnership) are two main venues for those negotiating efforts. Regulatory coherence was one of the key priorities. By 2016, prior to the US presidential election, TPP was agreed on and TTIP negotiations were making headway. The negotiating approach in TPP and TTIP was to find a common denominator as a focal point or a platform. Negotiating countries would realign their regulatory regime and practice along this common denominator. The key question is where to draw the line. The bigger the common denominator, the more enlarged the scope for common regulatory regime. The trade disciplines, which were negotiated under the US and the EU leadership, have been developed under this scheme. Just note agreements on Labor and Trade, Environment and Trade, State-Owned Enterprise, Competition, and E-Commerce in TPP.

China has been critical of this line of approach. From the standpoint of China, accepting the framework of standardization as a negotiating approach for deeper institutionalization means radical reform of its modus operandi. As long as China is hesitant on fundamentally restructuring the relationship between the state and the market, standardization cannot serve its trade liberalization template.

Despite its 2013 ambitious masterplan for economic reform, China has shown remarkable lapse in the implementation of its reform pledge. The lack of political will naturally translates into the Chinese, defensive stance on the standardization approach as Western conspiracy. As China is getting serious about making an exit from the reliance on Factory China, opening up and reform pursuant to the standardization approach has no place in its plan. The so-called Great Firewall of China, blocking free and open cyberspace for the Chinese people, illustrates what is at stake.

Reflecting all these internal constraints, China has been promoting so-called harmonization as its approach to deep integration. In dealing with different regulatory regimes in international trade and investment, China has adopted the strategy of "seek commonality and leave differences(求同存異)". The focus is not on "seek commonality" but on "leave differences." Whenever Beijing assesses its negotiating power to be weak, it speaks highly of "leave differences." Often, Beijing rephrased this tactic as "no interference with domestic affairs." In the West, this tactic is often translated as "agree to disagree." In essence, China's "seek commonality and leave differences" aims to maintain the status quo under strong external pressures to change it. In this regard, so-called harmonization is nothing more than the Chinese desire to keep its own course of action. As long as China maintains this negotiating approach, disparities in trade rules on the New Economy and key areas pertaining to the core features of the Chinese economy (such as SOE) would be hard to be reconciled.

Issues will not be easily settle unless China relaxes its control on its digital economy and SOEs. The US approach will not change either even after the Trump administration. China resorts to its captive domestic market for providing a strategic means to upscale local firms. The Great Firewall serves as a disguised trade barrier or industrial policy to promote local firms by excluding foreign firms. Considering the projection that China is unlikely to discard its strong control on digital cyberspace and SOEs, Korea and Japan will be given only one choice: Develop a common denominator between Japan and Korea, and make it de facto trade and investment platform in the region. Otherwise, face the unwieldy and assertive, yet powerful China.

4. Trajectories to 2030: Projection

For further institutionalization in Northeast Asia, critical missing links are the Korea-Japan trade agreement and the US-Japan trade agreement.

Korea-Japan FTA

Either as a pure bilateral trade agreement or as an integral part of Korea's accession to CPTPP, the Korea-Japan trade agreement can take place. Without a solid Korea-Japan trade agreement with comprehensive coverage and high-level commitment, none of the Bottom-up, Top-down, Out-in approach would lead to steps closer to deepening institutionalization in Northeast Asia.

The desirability of the Korea-Japan FTA may be elaborated on economic, political, and strategic dimensions. Korea and Japan mostly export raw materials and parts to Southeast Asian countries and manufacture them there to export the finished goods to advanced countries like the U.S. Japan, as a member of CPTPP, can capitalize on the supply chain of origin with other CPTPP members in Southeast Asia to further expand its exports market.

Talks on a bilateral agreement with Japan have been stalled since November 2004 due to strong domestic opposition. Opponents claim that striking a free trade pact with Japan would work unfavorably for Korea, with higher tariffs than Japan and still incurring large deficit in trade with the technology powerhouse. But this reasoning does not explain why Korea concluded FTAs separately with the United States and EU with much lower tariffs.

Local automakers could argue that the influx of cheaper Japanese cars could ruin domestic car sales. But they cannot rely forever on the government to cover up for them in a country that is the world's fifth-largest automobile producer. Actually, the Korean economy needs an FTA with Japan to make the local market more competitive and rationalize the inflated prices in the Korean market so as to benefit consumers. Korea has no reason to fear an FTA with Japan. Authorities must incorporate their vision of enhancing competition and consumers' rights into their trade strategy to pull Korea out of its deep-rooted phobia.

US-Japan FTA

To provoke and speed up the process of deep institutionalization, the preceding analysis also indicates the critical role of US-Japan FTA. The US-Japan FTA has been pursued by Washington since President Trump took the US out of the TPP. So far, the pressure from Washington has not been intense. Priorities have been on dealing with China. And, most of US negotiating resources are allocated to the renegotiation of NAFTA. In the midst of North Korea's intensified nuclear adventurism and unravelling of the TPP during the first year of Trump's presidency, the most remarkable development in Northeast Asia is the consolidation of US-Japan alliance. It is almost ironic. Japan spent its utmost effort to prevent Trump from wreaking TPP. Such a dire effort did not bear fruit. Ironically, all the efforts from the Japanese side began to build a new coalition between Tokyo and Washington. North Korea's accelerated path toward the completion of its nuclear capacity to strike the US continent also intensified the US-Japan alliance.

In this setting, one wonders why Tokyo remains reluctant and lukewarm to the idea of the US-Japan FTA. Japan is not the same country who hesitated to embrace comprehensive and high-level FTA due to its fear of the agriculture sector opening up. With the negotiations of TPP with the US, the negotiating stance of Japan has drastically improved. Japan de facto had a US-Japan FTA in the context of TPP. Moreover, Japan led to the establishment of CPTPP, which is TPP minus the US. It seems that Japan is spearheading the maintenance of the liberal order in the emergence of the New Normal. Japan is intent on attracting the US to CPTPP, which is the complete resurrection of TPP. Such U-turn from Washington may take place, Tokyo wants to believe. How long will it take? Not in the foreseeable future, as long as Trump emphasizes the magic of bilateralism on the new metric of reciprocal and fair trade. Hence, just waiting and waiting is not in the interest of Japan, if it is really serious about deepened institutionalization of trade relation in Northeast Asia in the era of the rise of assertive China. More strategic and forward-looking Japan would embrace the idea of the US-Japan FTA.

Prediction

Trajectories to Northeast Asia 2030 are variable geometry. Several pathways compete. Interplay between domestic factors and external factors would influence the likelihood and the speed of each pathway. Political leadership and strategy would favor a particular scenario against others. Main findings and implications from the scenario analysis are summarized as below.

1. CJK FTA negotiations will be protracted. The lack of visionary leadership, no sense of common destiny and shared prosperity stand in the way of progress.

2. As plan B, countries pursue their preferred game plan with a view to edging out the others. They play a non-cooperative game with all eyes on strategic preemption.

3. In plan B, CPTPP (TPP minus the US) stands out, while RCEP may come to the finish line sooner or later. Japan-led CPTPP preserves TPP in essence. RCEP may not serve as an effective platform for the next stage of deep liberalization in Northeast Asia. Then, the question becomes the place of Korea and China in the map of CPTPP.

4. In plan B, the missing link is the Korea-Japan FTA. Negotiations began in 2003 but was suspended a year later. Its prospect is not sanguine due to domestic politics and resistance from some suppliers. Nonetheless, domestic economic situations and external dynamics have drastically changed. Both Korea and Japan have become much more deeply involved in the comprehensive and high-level FTA with other major economies outside of Northeast Asia. Moreover, the platform for maintaining a liberal international economic order is established in CPTPP. De facto Korea

-Japan FTA may also take place in this context. This implies the Korea-Japan FTA is within reach, if there is a political will.

5. If Japan becomes strategic and forward looking, it may embrace the idea of a US-Japan FTA. A US-Japan FTA may set the next stage of deepening liberalization in motion. It may provoke Korea's entry into CPTPP, if the US becomes serious on returning to CPTPP. A trilateral FTA among the US, Japan, and Korea would be an imminent possibility as well.

6. Fragmentation is another likely scenario, if trade pessimism prevails. In this scenario, Japan is stuck in CPTPP, without making further strategic move to a US-Japan FTA. Korea does not actively pursue its membership in CPTPP, driven by anti-Japanese sentiment and domestic opposition to de facto Korea-Japan FTA.

7. China will continue to pursue its own game plan in the international stage. The Belt Road Initiative (BRI) backed by the AIIB will be steadily promoted as a new form of international, if not global, cooperation platform. BRI is all about China reaching out and going to the West. It is not connected to China's two most significant neighboring trade partners. Moreover, the BRI does not introduce significant principles for economic governance. China does not seek any standardization among different policies and regulations. Nor does it seek any common denominator. China keeps emphasizing harmonization among different polices. Consequences would be confusion, lack of transparency, and instability. Private network of influence (Quanxi) will be more important. Discretion of government officials will obstruct potentials. Conflict and disputes will be resolved by

power, not by rules. Northeast Asia will not find any strong impetus for deepening institutionalization.

8. The Role of the US: The absence of the US will be increasingly felt for the reform-minded policy makers in Northeast Asia. What if somehow the US rekindles its interest trade activism in East Asia? Such a rekindled trade activism may be the outcome of Trump's learning curve. After a year of pressure and appeasement tactics played on China in order to elicit China's support to deal with belligerent North Korea, the US may come to realize a growing necessity for a stronger pressure tactic. The US initiative for the US-Japan FTA is a case in point. In the first year into power, Trump was not ready to push forward the initiative strongly. With more experience and more learning, Trump would reassess the strategic map. If the US renews its pressure on Japan to launch the US Japan FTA talks, it would set in motion further dynamics for deep institutionalization.

9. What if China embarks on the second wave of reform and open?

President Xi, who came to power in 2012, is expected to stay in power beyond 2022 - exceeding the ordinary maximum ten-year term for a Chinese top leader. Xi is on the way to become the most powerful ruler since Deng Xiaoping, and closer to the status of Mao Zedong. Will Xi's strong grip on political power increase the likelihood of reform and opening up? Pessimistic predictions are running high. Growing numbers of China watchers turned critical of China's willingness of embarking on reforms as pledged in the 2013 Blueprint, the very first reform plan of Xi. To be fair to the Chinese leadership, the jury is still out. In case of China's serious implementation of reform, where market and private sector would play more critical roles in the Chinese economy, China will be at the driver's seat of deepening liberalization and upgrading institutionalization in Northeast Asia.

8 Future in the Making

Looming Confrontation

Thanks to its trade-oriented growth strategy, Northeast Asia has emerged as one of the most dynamic and vibrant economic regions in the world. The story of the rise of Northeast Asia is also the story of the rise of China. Embracing China into the global trading system has propelled the rise of China. As China continues to rise, expectation also runs high. Many around the world presume that more economic freedom and political freedom would be on the way. So far, such expectation has not been fulfilled. With consolidation of political power under the one person rule, the future direction of China is so interwoven with its relations to the world, including its neighbors and the US. Among multiplex equations of international political economy, the US-China relation is the most important, because the strategy of China's neighbors towards China derives from it.

Prior to the election of Trump as the US President, the relationship between the US and China has been more of cooperation and embracement. With the rise of the New Normal along with the arrival of Trump at the

White House, the US-China relationship has become more confrontational.

From the US point of view, China is an unfair and unruly country, while it freely roams around. The prevailing consensus in Washington is that China steals US technology, blocks US firms in its market, and outcompetes in the US market through subsidy, dumping, and currency manipulation.[90] With China within a striking distance of overtaking the US to be the most powerful country in the world, from the viewpoint of Beijing, policy makers and power elites in Washington seem determined to confront China. Filing complaints to the WTO would not be choice of the US. The US would deal with China one-on-one. The fact that the principal architect of multilateralism does not prefer to rely on the WTO signals the demise of multilateralism. Imposing punitive tariffs on Chinese products and blocking Chinese investments in the US would be main tools for the US. In the name of reciprocity, and also in the name of security concerns, unilateral pressures would be mounted.[91] China would not back down. Xi, whose secured no term limit as the supreme leader of China, would love to show the image of determination and

90 Both the Democratic Party and the Republican Party Platform of the 2016 Presidential election was full of China bashing. Also, refer to the USTR (2018a) on China's poor implementation record of its WTO commitment.

91 When Trump announced the imposition of steel and aluminum tariff in the name of security concern in March 2018, he opened the Pandora's box. Such trade sanction of particular products from all over the world under the security exception by the leading power has been rare, because such an act would break away from the well-established rule of the global trading system.

unyielding to the pressure from the ruling power to his people. China would retaliate against the US. At this point, the stage will be set for negotiated exit. What if negotiations fail? Then, the US may resort to even stronger punitive measures against China. Will that scare China? Further escalation may be waiting in the wings.

Clash between Washington and Beijing, and a possible outbreak of trade war between the US and China would spell serious repercussion to Korea and Japan alike. It is because the GVC of Factory China is structured around the supply of parts and components from Korea and Japan, which are assembled in China, destined to the US. How far will the US go? And how far will China go? Prolonged clash would take both Korea and Japan deeper into confusion and chaos. If clash between Washington and Beijing continues in a wide scope of products, Korea and Japan will confront the tough task of redrawing their GVC.

Alongside the looming trade war between the US and China, the rising tide of nationalism and populism in Northeast Asia is a growing concern. Unlike globalism, which pursues "mutually beneficial" outcome, nationalism is mainly about "I win - You lose." In particular, techno-nationalism of China is assured to be the most explosive agenda. China is determined to promote national champion in the designated fields of its strategic importance. In order to achieve its goals, China would not mind whether it violates or reneges on its commitment in the global trading system and bilateral trade agreements. Crumbled global trading system would not provide an effective venue to resolve trade disputes. Techno-nationalism may end up with the proliferation of a digital fortresses, which would take Northeast Asia to the downfall. Japan or Korea alone cannot stand up to the challenge. Well-coordinated approaches by Japan and Korea together may not be even outmatched for the task. This would call for the significance of bringing the US on board in Northeast Asia.

Case for Inclusive and Deep Integration

Two mega risks of the silver tsunami and disruptive technology are approaching Northeast Asia. Korea, Japan, and China race against time. The race of building a welfare society is set against the speed of the coming risks. Without an inclusive welfare society, sustainable growth will not be possible.

Japan should get out of the Lost Decades. Abenomics so far at least succeeded in breaking the psychology of depression. But shrinking population is driving Japan to the cliff. The country needs to move on fast from the cliff. Where will it find the source of speedy run away from the cliff?

Korea is caught in a class struggle between the labor force and the capitalists. Obsession with redistribution, without creating a new engine of growth, has been a recipe for disaster in many countries. Korean politicians seem ignorant of this historic tendency or overly confident that Korea will be different. Manufacturing-driven trade-oriented strategy has taken Korea to the ranks of advanced nations. Jobless growth and decreasing social mobility indicate that conventional strategy has reached its limit. If Korea fails to create a new engine for growth and transform its paradigm toward inclusive and sustained growth, the miracle story of Korea will be found in the history museum.

China at the moment is rejoicing its place under the sun: a super-sized economy with global reach. But rapidly accumulated debt, environmental degradation, and rising inequality threaten the future course of China. While Beijing understands the significance of efficient resource allocation, in particular financial capital, it would not want to give up its power at the driver's seat of running the economy. If China cannot manage deftly and shrewdly, it risks of falling in the middle income trap. Is there any way to enhance productivity without further opening up and reform?

Korea, Japan, and China face their own unique challenges and risks, and also common challenges and risks. Analysis of this book offers deep integration as a way to move forward: not deep integration in the frame of the so-called Washington consensus, but deep integration efforts in Northeast Asia to advance inclusive growth in the region. Without inclusive growth, the regime will be under the risk of losing power. Risk of losing power will run deep not only in democratic nations of Korea and Japan, but also in the socialist nation of China. Hence, deep integration without inclusive growth will not be politically unacceptable. Can a country achieve inclusive growth without deep integration? So far, no country has ever gone through that path. Growth through trade is what has taken Korea, Japan, and China this far. For sustained growth, the next step is to embark on the inclusive and deep integration, negotiating on agenda as suggested in 〈Table 22〉.

Table 22. Checklist for Inclusive and Deep Integration

1. Substantial tariff elimination
2. Reduction of Non-Tariff Barriers
3. Trade facilitation
4. Service: negative listing approach – service + manufacturing
5. Investment: CJK Investment agreement to be upgraded Market access + Investment protection
6. Movement of People
7. SOE in relation to competition and government procurement
8. Regulatory cooperation: Transparency, Coherence
9. Energy
10. Environment
11. Digital Trade

**Source: Choi 2016b

Cost of inaction

Consequences of the status quo or fragmentation without establishing a strong common platform for the New Economy in Northeast Asia would be enormously negative. Manufacturing-driven GVC in this region is under mounting pressure of reshaping. The region needs to ride the wave of disruptive technology, the so-called 4th Industrial Revolution. At the same time, headwinds of protectionism blowing from inside and outside of the region needs to be effectively addressed.

The absence of a common platform for deep integration will give rise to several risks. The rise of nationalism and populism in the region will disrupt and overtake ordinary management of economic activities. The Old Economy will be under inherent risk from trade-security linkage, as witnessed in China's trade retaliation in relation to the installation of

THAAD in Korea. The New Economy will suffer from the absence of a common platform. Economic activities in the New Economy will find themselves difficult to freely move beyond their national borders. Parallel to these risks, companies, investors, and other stakeholders will be under the threat of a power-based system. No matter how productive and successful a company may be, it could be an easy target for economic nationalism or populism. If players cannot play by the rules, then no one will accept the outcome. Northeast Asia, without a common platform, may turn into a jungle of the survival of the fittest.

Trade Entrepreneurship Imperative

A desirable path for the future of Northeast Asia is to establish a binding common interface for investment and services across national boundaries. To guide the Northeast Asian economy towards this path, three tasks are imperative. First, open up and expose these sectors to the force of fair competition. Second, reform these sectors prior to opening up to the outside. Otherwise, benefits from opening up would be collected by opportunistic rent seekers, not shared by small and medium, yet significant stakeholders. Reform should not mean reform along Western demands, as the IMF-imposed reform in the wake of the 1997 Asian Financial Crisis would attest. Third, pro-competitive policy framework needs to be adopted and constantly implemented. Anti-competitive behaviors, including attempts to monopolize the market, should be restrained under a legal framework.

Well-designed reform and opening up would facilitate the effective transformation of Northeast Asia from a major manufacturing powerhouse to a more balanced and sophisticated economic zone. Under the new platform of enhanced and coherent regulatory regime, common to all countries in Northeast Asia, aspiring young people and small business would be assured to have a fair chance of navigating their journey. It must be innovative entrepreneurs, not politically well-connected and powerful elites, who pick the fruits from this enhanced and enlarged platform. Consumers, not suppliers, will find their weight in this new frontier. A more forward-looking approach in the urgent areas of environmental degradation and exhaustible resources should be adopted. In these cross-cutting issues, the level of ambition should be lofty, not modest.

The case for deep integration in Northeast Asia is paramount. The cost of no action will rise over time. Even the biggest economy in the region cannot overcome the challenges of the changing times by itself. The silver tsunami of unprecedented scale and speed will swallow China, if China fails to make a transition to a service economy and build its own effective welfare society. Korea also faces the same challenge. While establishing a Korean-style welfare society is being delayed, the silver tsunami is getting closer to the shore. Korea not only lacks a social consensus on its vision of welfare society, but also faces the risk of diminishing budgets to build such a welfare society. Japan, the country which was swept by the silver tsunami the earliest in the region, is now experiencing the decline of its total population.

China, Japan, and Korea are racing against time. It would be mistake if a solid growth alone can distance the country from troubles. Without steady growth, financial resources to build a welfare society in the face of the silver tsunami would be embarrassingly inadequate. Finding a common framework for deep integration is tantamount to seek new sources of growth through innovation and through enhancing and scaling-up services.

Strategy to go forward

There is paramount importance of breaking ground for deeper institutionalization in Northeast Asia. However, the speed and scope of China's further and deeper liberalization, which would be instrumental for deeper institutionalization in the region, is likely to be slow, gradual, and incomprehensive. Despite its repeated rhetoric on the case for free trade and globalization, China seems lacking political commitment for the deep change. Given these circumstances, maintaining the usual course of action - business as usual - is not a way to go forward. Forward-looking and visionary trade activism is imperative. Shallow state of institutionalization and further delay in launching a new initiative towards deeper institutionalization would fulfill the prophecy of fragmentation, which would transform the vibrant and dynamic Northeast region into a static fortress.

A forward-looking strategy is to create the Korea-Japan-US FTA in the name of East Asian Economic Partnership (EAEP). Once the EAEP is up and running, it would serve the single most cohesive platform for service, investments, and trade rule in the New Economy. The EAEP also would generate tremendous momentum for further expansion. Eventually, China will face a binary choice: to join the common platform or to stay out. From strategic point of view, challenge is to make the choice of 'join' more attractive and compelling to China.

In case China decides to stay out, it may commit a mistake of enclosing its economy inside the wall. Considering so much interconnected nature of the Chinese economy with the global economy, such a seclusion would not serve the interest of China. Believing in its supersized domestic market, China's own emboldened nationalistic approach may repeat the mistake of Japan in the 1990s, when Japan decided to play with its own local standard incompatible with the global one in its attempt to fend off the foreign competitors. Back then, the Japanese economy was the second largest economy in the world, on the verge of overtaking the US economy. Too much confidence in its domestic market, the Japanese policy makers came up with protective and defense strategy. What has happened ever since was the lackluster performance of the Japanese economy. Those sectors the Japanese policy makers tried to protect from the global competition were trapped inside of Japan.

Will China prove different? China's reliance on key parts and components from Korea, Japan and the US is stronger than the Japanese case in the 1990s. Overcoming this critical reliance through the Chinese industrial policy under the veil of economic nationalism is assuredly to be costly. Trade disputes with the US will be more frequent. China's access to the US may be severely undermined. China will lose its biggest market for its consumer products and the source of acquiring technology and brand.

China would look for compromise, not confrontation to the end.

If China decides to join the common platform of the EAEP, Northeast Asia will have a shared platform, which would also be reinforced by the presence of the US. As for China, the value of joining the EAEP is not simply the economic benefit of getting connected in the era of digital transformation. The EAEP would also create the vital strategic value to China. By embracing the vision of the EAEP, China could break away from its unwanted image as 'sharp power', which will be a pivotal step for China's ambition as a regional power. Can China see through economic and strategic value of the EAEP? Can Korea, Japan, and the US imagine and champion the vision of the EAEP? Whether the Northeast forges ahead and drifts away depends on the answers to these questions.

References

Abe, Shinzho. 2015 "Toward an Alliance of Hope" Address to a Joint Meeting of the U.S. Congress by Prime Minister Shinzo Abe, April 30.

Acemoglu, Daron and James Robinson. 2012. *Why Nation Fail: The Origins of Power, Prosperity, and Poverty*, Crown Business. New York.

Ahn Hyungdo and Jehoon Park. 2007. *A Political-economic Approach to Northeast Asian Regional Cooperation: Search for a New Model and Korea's Strategies*, Korea Institute for International Economic Policy (in Korean)

Allison, Graham T. 2017. *Destined for War: Can America and China Escape Thucydides's Trap?*, Boston: Houghton Mifflin Harcourt.

Allison, Graham and Robert Blackwill. 2013. *Lee Kuan Yew: The Grand Master's Insights on China, the United States, and the World*. The MIT Press.

Autor, David. 2014. "Skills, Education, and the Rise of Earnings Inequality among the 'Other 99 Percent'" *Science*, Vol 344, May: 843-51

Autor, David, David Dorn, and Gordon H. Hanson. 2013. "The China Syndrome: Local Labor Market Effects of Import Competition in the United States" *American Economic Review*, Vol 103(6): 2121–2168

__________. 2016. "The China Shock: Learning from Labor Market Adjustment to Large Changes in Trade" NBER Working Paper No. 21906

Baldwin, Richard. 2016. *The Great Convergence*, Belknap Press, November.

Barfield, Claude. 2011. "Telecoms and Huawei Conundrum: Chinese Foreign Direct Investment in the United States" AEI Economic Studies

__________. 2016. "How Trump's trade policy is dividing Republicans" 28 July.AEI.

Bergsten and et al. 2008. *China's Rise: Challenges and Opportunities*, Peterson Institute for International Economics.

Bergsten, C. Fred . 2008. "A Partnership of Equals" *Foreign Affairs, July*/August

Bhagwati, Jagdish 1988. *Protectionism*. The MIT Press.

Bremmer, Ian. 2010. *The End of the Free Market: Who Wins the War Between States and Corporation?* The Penguin Press

Brynjolfsson, Erik and Andrew McAfee. 2011. *Race against the Machine: How the Digital Revolution is Accelerating Innovation, Driving Productivity, and Irreversibly Transforming Employment and the Economy*. Digital Frontier Press.

Campbell, Kurt and Ely Ratner. 2018. "The China Reckoning: How Beijing Defied American Expectations" *Foreign Affairs*, January/February

China File. 2013. "Document 9: A China File Translation" November 8. http://www.chinafile.com/document-9-chinafile-translation

Choi, Byung-il. 2005. "Mad for Garlic: Domestic Politics of Trade Dispute" in Choi, Byung-il ed 2005 *Korea and International Conflicts: Case Studies*, Volume 1. Institute for International Trade and Cooperation

____________. 2006. *The KORUS FTA: Against the All Odds*. Seoul: Random House. (in Korean)

____________. 2009. *The KORUS FTA at crossroads: A Solution*. Seoul: Joongang Books. (in Korean)

____________. 2014. *A Nation Haunted by the 1%: Rebuilding the Korean Economy*. Seoul. Free Economy Books. (in Korean)

____________. 2015. "The Evolution of China's International Trade Relations and the Future" in *China, New Paradigm*, Korea Foundation for Advanced Studies, Seoul: Hanwool Academy (in Korean)

____________. 2016a "Whither the TPP? Political Economy of Ratification and Effect on Trade Architecture in East Asia" *East Asian Economic Review* Vol. 20(3), September: 311 338

____________. 2016b. *Paths and Strategies towards the FTAAP: Linking Integration and Inclusive Growth*, APEC Study Series 16-01, November. Korea Institute for International Economic Policy.

____________. 2017. "The State of Global Economy and G20" G20 Conference, Seoul, December 5, 2017.

Choi, Byung-il and Bora Joo. 2016. "A Tale of Two Reforms: Korea vs. Greece - Political economy of reform under crisis", *Korea Observer*, Vol. 47(1).

Choi, Byung-il and Kyounghee Lee. 2013. "Future of Trading Architecture in Asia Pacific: TPP vs. RCEP", *KERI Brief*.

Choi, Byung-il and Jennifer Oh. 2011. "Asymmetry in Japan and Korea's Agricultural Liberalization in FTA: Domestic Trade Governance Perspective" *Pacific Review*, Vol. 24(5): 505-527.

________________________. 2017. "Reversed Asymmetry in Japan's and Korea's FTAs: TPP and Beyond", *Pacific Focus*, Vol. 32(2).

Choi, Byung-il and Changyoung Rhee. 2014. *Future of Factory Asia*, Asia Development Bank and Korea Economic Research Institute.

Choi, Seokyoung. 2016. *A Diplomat's Journal on Korea's FTA Negotiations*, Seoul: Pakyoungsa. (in Korean).

Chun Hongtack and Myung-Ho Park. 2011. *Integration Strategy for East Asia: Focusing on Korea, China and Japan*, Korea Development Institute. (in Korean)

CSIS. 2013. China's Competitiveness: Myths, Realities and Lessons for the US and Japan, Center for Strategic and International Studies.

Davis, Bob and Jon Hilsenrath (2016) "How the China Shock, Deep and Swift, Spurred the Rise of Trump" August 11. The Wall Street Journal. https://www.wsj.com/articles/how-the-china-shock-deep-and-swift-spurred-the-rise-of-trump-1470929543

Democratic Party. 2016. 2016 Democratic Party Platform. https://www.demconvention.com/wp-content/uploads/2016/07/Democratic-Party-Platfor-7.21.16-no-lines.pdf

Chen, Celia and Iris Deng. 2018. "WeChat joins list of Chinese technology banned by overseas militaries on security worries" *South China Morning Post*. March 15. http://www.scmp.com/tech/china-tech/article/2137232/wechat-joins-list-chinese-technology-banned-overseas-militaries

Dickson, Bruce. 2016. *The Dictator's Dilemma: The Chinese Communist Party's Strategy for Survival*, New York, Oxford University Press.

Duhigg, Charles and Keith Bradsher. 2012. "*How the U.S. Lost Out on iPhone Work*" *New York Times*. January 22. https://www.nytimes.com/2012/01/22/business/apple-america-and-a-squeezed-middle-class.html

Eichengreen, Barry, Dwight Perkins and Kwanho Shin. 2012. *From Miracle to Maturity: The Growth of the Korean Economy*, Harvard University Asia Center.

Forbes. 2015. "At $68 Billion Valuation, Uber Will Be Bigger Than GM, Ford, And Honda". Dec 4, 2015.

______. 2018. "Breaking Down Uber's Valuation: An Interactive Analysis"

Friedman, Thomas. 1999. *The Lexus and the Olive Tree: Understanding Globalization*. Farrar, Straus and Giroux.

______________. 2017. "Trump is a Chinese Agent" New York Times. March 29.

Froman, Michael. 2015. "We are at the end of the line on the Doha Round of trade talks" Financial Times. December 13.

Gilpin, Robert 1987. *The Political Economy of International Relations*. Princeton

University Press.

Glawe, Linda and Helmut Wagner. 2017. "The People's Republic of China in the Middle-income Trap?" ADBI Working Paper Series, No. 749 June 2017.

Gordon, Bernard. 2012 "Trading Up in Asia: Why the United States Need the Trans Pacific Partnership?" *Foreign Affairs. July/*August.

Gordon, Robert J. 2016. *The Rise and Fall of American Growth: The U.S. Standard of Living Since the Civil War*, Princeton University Press.

Hall and Soskice. 2001. *Varieties of Capitalism: The Institutional Foundations of Comparative Advantage*, Oxford University Press.

Hahm, Chaibong. 2017. "Keeping Northeast Asia "Abnormal": Origins of the Liberal International Oder in Northeast Asia and the New Cold War" Open Forum, Asan Institute for Policy Studies. September 11.

Hicks, Michael J. and Srikant Devaraj. 2015. "The Myth and the Reality of Manufacturing in America" *Center for Business and Economic Research*, Ball State University.

Hornbeck, J. 2013. "Trade Adjustment Assistance and Its Role in U.S. Trade Policy" Congressional Research Service.

Huang, Echo and Isabella Steger. 2017. "Beijing's Long Arm: Forced to comply or shut down, Cambridge University Press's China Quarterly removes 300 articles in China" *Quartz*. August 18. https://qz.com/1056938/cambridge-university-press-china-quarterly-complies-with-censorship-removes-300-articles-on-topics-like-tiananmen-and-tibet-in-china/

Huang, Q., G. Liu, J. He, F. Jiang, and Y. Huang. 2017. Middle-Income Trap and Manufacturing Transformation of the People's Republic of China (PRC): Asian Experience and the PRC's Industrial Policy Orientation. ADBI Working Paper 752. Tokyo: Asian Development Bank Institute.

Huang, Yukon. 2017. Cracking the China Conundrum: *Why Conventional Economic Wisdom Is Wrong*, Oxford University Press

Irvine, Roger. 2016. *Forecasting China's Future: Dominance or Collapse?*, London, Routledge.

Jwa, Sung-Hee. 2017. *A General Theory of Economic Development: Towards a Capitalist Manifesto*. Edward Elgar.

Kissinger, Henry. 2011. *On China*, The Penguin Press.

Lardy, Nicholas R. 2012. *Sustaining China's Economic Growth After the Global Financial Crisis*, Peterson Institute for International Economics.

Lee, Jessica J. . 2015. "The Truth about South Korea's TPP Shift," *The Diplomat* October 23.

Li, Eric X, 2017. "Under Xi, a Chinese renaissance is assured, contrary to what the West believes", South China Morning Post, November 1

Mahbubani, Kishore. 2013. *The Great Convergence: Asia, the West, and the Logic of One World*, Public Affairs.

McKinsey Global Institute. 2013. *Beyond Korean Style: Shaping a New Growth Formula.*

Mearsheimer, John. 2014. *Tragedy of the Great Power Politics.* Updated edition. W.W. Norton & Company.

_______________. 2014. "Can China Rise Peacefully?" The National Interest, October 25.

Milanovic, Branko. 2016. "Why the Global 1% and the Asian Middle Class Have Gained the Most from Globalization", Harvard Business Review, May.

Milanovic, Branko and Christoph Lakner. 2013. "Global Income Distribution: From the Fall of the Berlin Wall to the Great Recession", *Policy Research Working Paper*, The World Bank Development Research Group, December.

Moon, Jae-in. 2017. "Handshaking of the Youth of Korea and China: The Future of Prosperity in the Common Endeavor" Speech at Peiking University. December 15.

Nakagawa, Junji . 2014. "CJK FTA's role in developing investment framework in and beyond CJK" presented at the Third CJK FTA Seminar, November 26, Tokyo, Japan.

Naughton, Barry. 2006. *The Chinese Economy: Transition and Growth*, MIT Press.

Nye, Joseph S. 1999. "As China Rises, Must Others Bow?," *Economist*, June 25

Pei, Minxin. 2016. *China's Crony Capitalism: The Dynamics of Regime Decay*, Cambridge, MA, Harvard University Press.

Petri, Peter and Michael Plummer. 2016. "The Economic Effects of the Trans-Pacific Partnership: New Estimates." Working Paper Series 16 (2). Peterson Institute for International Economics.

Pettis, Michael. 2013. *Avoiding the Fall: China's Economic Restructuring*, Carnegie Endowment for International Peace, Brookings Institution Press

Phillusbury, Michael. 2016. *The Hundred-Year Marathon: China's Secret Strategy to Replace America as the Global Superpower*, St. Martin's Griffin.

Pritchett, Lant and Lawrence H. Summers. 2014. "Asiaphoria Meets Regression to the

Mean" NBER Working Paper No. 20573, October.

Putnam, Robert. 1988. "Diplomacy and Domestic Politics: The Logic of Two-Level Games" *International Organization*. Vol. 42, No. 3, Summer, pp. 427-460

Rein, Shaun. 2014. *The End of Cheap China,* Wiley

Republican Party. 2016. Republican Party Platform 2016. (URL: https://www.gop.com/the-2016-republican-party-platform/ , accessed July 31, 2016)

Riordan, Primrose and Rowan Callick. 2017 "China consulate involved in Newcastle Uni Taiwan row" *The Australian*. August 28. https://www.theaustralian.com.au/national-affairs/china-consulate-involved-in-newcastle-uni-taiwan-row/news-story/14dceb31c1e72807c9f006936784c601

Schaede, Ulrike. 2004. "What Happened to the Japanese Model?" *Review of International Economics* Vol 12(2), May: 277-294.

Schott, Jeffrey and Cathleen Cimino 2015 "The China-Japan-Korea Trilateral Investment Agreement: Implications for US Policy and the US-China Bilateral Investment Treaty" in *Towards A US-China Investment Treaty*. PIIE Briefing 15-1. Peterson Institute for International Economics.

Scollay, Robert. 2016. "FTAAP and Its Pathways: State of Play and Ways Forward" Paper presented at the APEC Study Center Consortium Conference, Arequipa, Peru. May 4-5

Shambaugh, David. 2016. *China's Future*, Cambridge, UK, Malden, MA, Polity Press

________________. 2017. "Reform or repression: what will the next five years bring for China?" *South China Morning Post*, October 12.

Sim, Walter. 2018 "TPP-11 deal a major boost to Pacific Rim economies' The Strait Times. Jan 23. https://www.straitstimes.com/asia/east-asia/tpp-11-deal-a-major-boost-to-pacific-rim-economies

Solis, Mireya. 2016. "The high stakes of TPP ratification: Implications for Asia-Pacific and beyond" March 10, 2016, Brookings Institution.Spence, Michael. 2011. *The Next Convergence: The Future of Economic Growth in a Multispeed World*, Picador.

Takashi, Terada. 2015. "Japan and the TPP Conclusion: Regional Order, Negotiations, and Domestic Adjustment," *The Asan Forum* October 23.

US Congress. 2002. Bipartisan Trade Promotion Authority Act of 2002. https://www.congress.gov/bill/107th-congress/house-bill/3009/text

USTR. 2012. "The United States Concludes Review of Model Bilateral Investment Treaty" April.

_____. 2016. The Trans-Pacific Partnership: Full Text

______ 2017a. "Opening Plenary Statement of USTR Robert Lighthizer at the WTO MinisterialConference". https://ustr.gov/about-us/policy-offices/press-office/press -releases/2017/december/opening-plenary-statement-ustr

______ 2017b. "USTR Robert Lighthizer Statement on the Conclusion of the WTO MinisterialConference" https://ustr.gov/about-us/policy-offices/press-office/press-releases/ 2017/december/ustr-robert-lighthizer-statement

______. 2018a. 2017 *Report to Congress on China's WTO Compliance*

______. 2018b. "New U.S. Trade Policy and National Security Outcomes with the Republic of Korea" USTR. March 28, 2018. https://ustr.gov/about-us/policy-offices/press-office/fact-sheets/2018/march/new-us-tr ade-policy-and-national

Vogel, Steven. K. 2006. *Japan Remodeled: How Government and Industry are Reforming Japanese Capitalism*, Cornell University

Wade, Robert. 1990. *Governing the Market*, Princeton University Press.

Walker, Christopher and Jessica Ludwig. 2017. "From 'Soft Power' to 'Sharp Power': Rising Authoritarian Influence in the Democratic World" in *Sharp Power*, National Endowment for Democracy.

Walter, Carl E. and Fraser Howie. 2011. *Red Capitalism: The Fragile Financial Foundation of China's Extraordinary Rise*, Wiley.

Wang, Jisi. 2011. "China's Search for a Grand Strategy: A Rising Great Power Finds Its Way" *Foreign Affairs*, Vol. 90, No. 2. March/April.

Washington Post. 2016."How the TPP became the most divisive policy in the Democratic Party". July 26.

Xinhua 2007. "Premier: China Confident in Maintaining Growth" March 16 http://www.china.org.cn/english/2007lh/203252.htm

White House. 2016. "Statement by the President on the Signing of the Trans-Pacific Partnership" Feb 3.

Xi Jinping. 2017. speech at the Davos Forum, January 17.

Yoshimatsu, Hidetaka 2015 "Locating Japanese Trade Policy in an Evolving Regional Context" in *The Political Economy of Japanese Trade Policy*, edited by Aurelia Mulgan and Masayoshi Honma, Palgrave Macmillan

Zoellick, Robert. 2005. "Whither China: From Membership to Responsibility?" Remarks to National Committee on US-China Relations, New York City, September 21.

Abstract

Notwithstanding political asymmetry among the nations, the interplay of globalization and national strategy has transformed Northeast Asia as one of the most vibrant and prosperous economic zones in the world. The spectacular rise of Northeast Asia in the global footprint has accompanied the rise of China from the largest poor nation to the world factory. By 2030, barring major crisis, China would have become or about to become the largest economy in the world, overtaking the US.

As the rise of China continues, China is getting more assertive on its own interest, disregarding the existing rules of the game. China's trade retaliation on the deployment of THAAD in Korea is a case in point. The fiasco laid bare rather fragile institutional foundation and the inherent risk of trade architecture of Northeast Asia. Without strengthening institutional foundation and upgrading trade architecture, the future navigation of Northeast Asia confronts so much uncertainties and risks.

Will Northeast Asia forge ahead with common interface or drift away with fragmentation? This book is an attempt to project future trajectories of economic architecture of Northeast Asia by 2030. In projecting future trajectories of economic architecture of Northeast Asia by 2030, two trade games are analyzed with historical evolution and strategic interaction: the contest between China, the rising power, and the US, the incumbent power; and the contest between China and its neighbor countries of Korea and

Japan.

For Factory China to be operational and lead Northeast Asia to its remarkable economic achievement, the nexus of ideology-institution-technology was critical. Advance of new digital technological breakthrough and the headwinds of economic nationalism, however, have disrupted such a long-standing nexus. Moreover, the election of Trump and consolidating power of Xi have pushed the world to the uncharted territory of "New Normal", where rule-based free trade is giving into power-based managed trade. Using the two-level perspective, the book analyzes the main features of "New Normal" and discusses its consequences on Northeast Asia.

In the light of the surge of nationalism and populism with the receding globalism, policy makers face the daunting challenge of inclusive yet deeper institutionalization. The future trajectory of Northeast Asia is closely tied to the speed and scope of China's further and deeper liberalization and reform, which is likely to be slow, gradual, and incomprehensive. Hence, forward-looking and visionary trade activism is in need. Status quo and further delay in embarking on inclusive and deeper institutionalization would fragment trading architecture of Northeast Asia. This book identifies policy options for inclusive and deeper institutionalization, and comes up with grand strategies for moving forward.

ARI Monograph Series 31

Northeast Asia in 2030: Forging Ahead or Drifting Away?

First Published 2018

by The Asiatic Research Institute at Korea University
145 Anam-ro, Seongbuk-gu, Seoul 136-701, Korea
www.asiaticresearch.org

Price : 19,000 won
ISBN : 979-11-89273-04-0 94300
ISBN : 978-89-90769-29-9 (SET)